Tracking

Controversial Issues in Education

Tracking: Conflicts and Resolutions
Character Education or Indoctrination: Whose Values?
Debating National Standards
Gender Equity in Schools
Gifted and Talented Education: Needed or Not?
Inclusion Issues for Schools
Interdisciplinary Curriculum

Tracking

Conflicts and Resolutions

Anne Turnbaugh Lockwood

CORWIN PRESS, INC.
A Sage Publications Company
Thousand Oaks, California

For information address:

Corwin Press, Inc.
A Sage Publications Company
2455 Teller Road
Thousand Oaks, California 91320
e-mail: order@corwin.sagepub.com

SAGE Publications Ltd.
6 Bonhill Street
London EC2A 4PU
United Kingdom

SAGE Publications India Pvt. Ltd.
M-32 Market
Greater Kailash I
New Delhi 110 048 India

Printed in the United States of America

Library of Congress Cataloging-in-Publication Data

Lockwood, Anne Turnbaugh.
    Tracking: conflicts and resolutions / Anne Turnbaugh Lockwood.
        p. cm. — (Controversial issues in education)
    Includes bibliographical references (pp. 66-68)
    ISBN 0-8039-6480-3 (cloth : alk. paper). — ISBN 0-8039-6268-1
(pbk. : alk. paper)
     1. Track system (Education)   I. Title. II. Series.
LB3061.8.L63   1996
371.2'54—dc20
                                              96-28060

This book is printed on acid-free paper.

96 97 98 99 00 10 9 8 7 6 5 4 3 2 1

Corwin Press Production Editor: S. Marlene Head

Contents

Acknowledgments

In particular, I would like to thank Adam Gamoran, Roger Genest, Anna Hunderfund, Reba Neukom Page, and Anne Wheelock for their willingness to scrutinize the issue of tracking one more time through the lens of my questions. I am grateful for their time, comments, and helpful suggestions for revision.

I also am indebted to Anne Wheelock for her generous suggestions and nominations of practitioners to interview for possible inclusion in this book.

And as always, I thank my husband, Alan L. Lockwood, for his ongoing, generous support and encouragement.

ANNE TURNBAUGH LOCKWOOD

.

About the Author

Anne Turnbaugh Lockwood is an Honorary Fellow in the Department of Curriculum and Instruction at the University of Wisconsin—Madison. Her work, which focuses on diminishing the barriers between educational research and practice, has been recognized by the American Educational Research Association Interpretive Scholarship Award (1993) and the Distinguished Achievement Award of the University of Wisconsin's School of Education (1993). The author of *Conversations with Educational Leaders: Contemporary Viewpoints on Education in America* (to be published Spring 1997 by SUNY Press), she also produced two nationally respected programs of publications targeted to educational researchers and practitioners: first, for the U.S. Department of Education's National Center on Effective Secondary Schools (1986–1990) and second, for the National Center for Effective Schools (1990–1994), both at the University of Wisconsin—Madison. In addition, she consults as a senior writer and policy analyst for the U.S. Department of Education's North Central Regional Educational Laboratory (Oak Brook, Illinois). She holds a Ph.D. in educational psychology from the University of Illinois at Urbana—Champaign.

Introduction

I first became aware of the social effects of tracking as a freshman in high school—a small, severely stratified school located in the Chicago suburbs. When growing up closer to the city in a primarily working-class, all-white community, I attended a K–8 elementary school where I was familiar with my classmates' abilities. Although their abilities differed, in other aspects they were remarkably similar. Most male parents worked at a local factory and did not have college educations; most mothers were homemakers. For the most part, we all dressed similarly; although my father was an administrator in the school district, overall there were no egregious differences in our families' income levels.

Typical of many elementary schools, we were grouped in reading within the classroom at times and not at other times. Whether or not we were grouped, we all knew—surely and inexorably—which students had trouble with reading, who was slow, who took so long sounding out words that some of us would roll our eyes at each other, who was a star. Yet we were all together in the same classroom, and the student who did not shine in reading might display a pronounced affinity for science or math. In other words, the effects of our reading groups seemed to even themselves out.

Yet this is not to say that reading groups—and later, math groups—did not have their own pernicious effects. I saw classmates' confidence falter as they were repeatedly assigned to low groups or demoted from a high group to a low group.

Demotion was especially devastating, as it was usually public, and accompanied by jeers. Depending on how strongly the teacher interceded, within-class grouping, as I experienced it—and my experiences are probably quite typical—could be relatively benign or more laden with issues of self-esteem, confidence, motivation, and a sense of self-efficacy.

Although my elementary school experience wasn't always pleasant, the social stratification ushered in by my freshman year of high school was a completely different experience. I was tracked into all honors classes, with the baffling exception of science. Although I couldn't pretend any advanced knowledge of or interest in science, to this day I do not know how the decision was made to place me in "general biology"—I suspect something as mundane as a scheduling snafu or an actual mistake.

My first day in the class, I was taken aback by what I saw when I looked at the other students. Somehow, although I had completed eighth grade in the district's junior high, I had never noticed them before. They were the shadowy students who were always on the fringes, never in activities, certainly not in my classes—which were filled with potential honors students: the sons and daughters of the local physicians, corporate executives, and attorneys. My peers in general biology were the students who didn't have "cool" clothes, judged by the narrow standards of the time—and had perfected the art of invisibility. Always on the periphery of school action, they clumped in their own small groups on the sidelines without participating in sports or any other extracurricular activities that, technically, were open to anyone.

A few words of explanation help set the social context for the high school: The community was and remains small, with an approximate population of less than 10,000. One of the last stops on the commuter train from Chicago, it is home to a variety of business and corporate executives and CEOs; its country club at that time was a singular social focus for the parents of many, if not most, of the honors students. Whether or not one's parents belonged to "the club" was a mark of enormous social distinction in the school. It was and is a community that prides itself on its resemblance to small, affluent Connecticut suburbs. Careful zoning and the use of picturesque old houses as sites for local businesses contributed to this image. When I was introduced to the short stories of John Cheever and his dark portraits of affluent Connecticut suburbs, I recognized the town in which I attended high school.

General biology could have been called anything, for all I would have known. What made it "general"—and clearly substandard, both socially and academically—was the presence of the shadowy students I had never noticed before and the choice of instructor. Although students dressed in a presentable way, clearly they did not have the benefit of any "extras." Some of them were not quite clean, certainly not up to the hygienic standards that the popular Breck shampoo commercials of the time exemplified. Surprisingly, they were very friendly to me—considerably friendlier than the honors students in my other classes, who viewed me with a certain degree of disdain. My parents, after all, did not belong to the country club, I was a relative newcomer from an unpretentious community, and social cliques were long-standing and had been established in elementary school. The classroom atmosphere in general biology was considerably cozier than the chilly atmosphere of my other classes.

I don't remember much about the quality of instruction in the class except it was painfully apparent to all of us that we had been assigned a teacher who was definitely not in the upper echelon of his peers. He seemed just as much an outcast as the rest of us, although he was pleasant and tried to engage us in lab activities. Still, everyone in the school knew he was not one of the better teachers, and worse, we could sense that he knew it himself. As a result, a certain dispirited quality permeated the class.

I discovered after a few weeks of class that an even lower tier of science existed, a fact revealed to me when a classmate in general biology explained the sorting system to me one day by saying, "That class is for the *really* dumb kids." The most astonishing part of the school's tracking system was the fact that most of the honors students didn't seem aware of its existence. Even though most adolescents are solipsistic, it was the lower-track students who understood the tracking system, almost intuitively, and how it worked.

Although many years have passed since general biology, I probably remember it more clearly than most of my other high school classes because of the feeling of entering another world—a world that I abandoned when I left the class. We talked among ourselves much more than in other classes—without sanctions for doing so—and I learned that students had modest career aspirations for themselves and what seemed to me to be a depressing, spiritless acceptance of their futures. Almost none planned to attend college or community college, nor did they express any desire to do so. When they talked about school, it was apparent that they looked forward to "getting out." Some even discussed with me the pros and cons of dropping out—a topic that filled me with horror because it was such an alien concept.

When they revealed where they lived, I discovered that people with faces and names lived in the small, extremely modest houses that dotted the otherwise affluent picture of the town. Their parents did not commute to Chicago to well-paid jobs; instead, most of them worked in a local factory that manufactured batteries. They talked about how they would work there too, after graduating from high school. Some of the young women stated that rather than work at the factory, they wanted to get married and have babies.

Equally disturbing—and distinctly odd to me at the time—was their acknowledgment that I would have a different future, a future that would include college and opportunities not available to them. They accepted this, and they accepted me. At the time, I found it embarrassing that in such a matter-of-fact way they slotted themselves into a relatively drab future but were careful not to include me in their vision. When they occasionally made a remark about "the rich kids," we all knew to whom they were referring—and none of us were in that company. And although they were friendly to me in class, the social lines were definite and tightly drawn. One young woman once remarked to me that although it would be fun to do something together outside school, "It wouldn't work out."

Although we shared a certain degree of friendship, even intimacy, in the class, once we were released into the halls, things changed. When I would pass my general biology peers in the halls, usually they would avert their eyes as if we had a tacit understanding that we only knew each other in that experience that had been compelled by the school. In other words, they knew their place—and they knew mine, sad as it is to acknowledge more than 25 years later.

Why should my personal recollections about the effects of tracking matter? Why do I recount these impressionistic memories in the context of a book on the school practices of tracking and ability grouping? Doesn't everyone have experiences they could recount—much worse, with long-lasting ramifications?

I introduce this book with my personal account because, to a large degree, people remember how they were placed and valued in school. This memory is highly personal and usually indelible. To some degree it probably explains the intensity with which many approach their class reunions. People do remember—sometimes with startling clarity—how institutions such as schools rated their abilities, valued their accomplishments, and sorted them for their futures. The point of my rather naive encounter with one suburban, relatively affluent high school's treatment of issues related to social class is that my story illustrates but one of an infinite number of responses to tracking, grouping, and sorting experiences.

The purpose of this monograph is to offer both the viewpoints of researchers who have grappled with the issue of tracking and the personal experiences of school staff who have wrestled with the issue of whether or not to track instruction. I decided to extend these perspectives to the reader through a genre I have been developing for the past several years: interviews and conversations with educational figures from both research and practice. Through these interviews, educators relate their perspectives and experiences in a way that is different from their conference presentations and research papers. It is the goal of this book that these selected views and experiences will focus more sharply the complexities of the tracking issue through the words of those most intimately engaged in its consideration.

I chose the researchers from their published writings and my own knowledge of their work, and the practitioners from the recommendations of Anne Wheelock, who has worked extensively with school staff nationwide on the issue of detracking schools (documented in her book, *Crossing the Tracks: How "Untracking" Can Save*

America's Schools). Each was contacted and agreed to participate in this project; each then was interviewed by phone. These interviews were tape-recorded; I then worked from a transcript to re-create our conversation. Each individual read the final product and made suggestions for the sake of clarity and refinement.

A word of explanation about my role: I asked open-ended questions in an effort to treat the issue as even-handedly as possible, although I am opposed to tracking for fundamental reasons related to the meaning of democracy and the ideals of public education. As a result of my style of questioning, my role in the interviews is somewhat muted: I deliberately played down my own reactions and attitudes so that the reader will focus on the voices and experiences of the interviewees.

The researchers included in this book are Adam Gamoran, Professor of Sociology and Educational Policy Studies at the University of Wisconsin—Madison; Reba Neukom Page, Visiting Associate Professor of Education at Harvard University and an Associate Professor at the University of California, Riverside; and Anne Wheelock, an advocate for detracking schools who is based in Massachusetts and Vermont.

The two practitioners come from different perspectives and settings. First we hear from Roger Genest, a veteran English teacher and English department chair at Pioneer Valley Regional High School in Northfield, Massachusetts. Pioneer Valley is a small, rural consolidated high school with a relatively homogeneous student population that draws from four surrounding communities. Genest originally was protracking in the belief that it was the only way to meet the differing abilities of students. Today, he is an outspoken advocate for heterogeneous grouping—primarily because of the benefits that accrued to his own instructional practices.

Second, Anna Hunderfund, Assistant to the Superintendent for Curriculum and Instruction in the Jericho Union Free School District in Jericho, New York, talks about the pressure on Jericho's students to perform. Although Jericho's student population appears to be homogeneous, the twin pressures of affluence and high expectations make it the type of community within which one could expect tracking to be an entrenched and unquestioned practice.

Hunderfund describes the shift she facilitated to heterogeneous grouping, on the one hand, and from a traditional junior high for Grades 6–8 to a research-based middle school propelled, above all, by the developmental needs of middle-school-aged youngsters.

Although each of these individuals has an distinct perspective on the topic, certain themes permeate all the views collected in this volume.

Tracking, considered in isolation from instruction and curriculum as a purely structural practice, is not the real issue facing schools: Instead, more complex and difficult questions related to curriculum and instruction are the more substantive and difficult problems with which schools must contend. As each researcher and practitioner in this monograph will attest, it is much more difficult to improve the quality of instruction than it is simply to make a decision that schools will detrack their instruction. The most successful instances of detracking, as the practitioners will show, occur when the decision is made carefully, over a period of time, with the ultimate goal of not only enhancing equity for all students but improving the quality of what they learn and how they learn it.

Arguments about whether or not to track instruction further polarize districts and communities and can lead to a climate in which nothing productive related to bettered curriculum and instruction will be achieved. In a tense, polarized community that huddles around two ends of the spectrum—either "We must track" or "We cannot track"—the importance of what and how children learn is lost, or at least obscured. The more stubbornly people cling to their positions and try to win others over to their points of view, the more acrimonious the debate becomes until it is an end in and of itself.

Heterogeneous instruction does not mean that students with poor academic backgrounds are left to flounder; it also does not mean that the brightest students carry the burden of learning for the others. Common misconceptions about heterogeneous instruction include the belief that low-achieving students will be left adrift without any attention to their needs and that high-achieving students will be unchallenged. As Anne Wheelock points out, such need not be the case. In carefully constructed heterogeneous groups of learners, high-achieving students profit from diverse points of view, learn how to articulate their own arguments, and benefit intellectually from the free exchange of ideas with other students. When heterogeneous instruction "works," it does not hold back advanced students— nor should it.

Heterogeneous instruction does not mean everyone should be treated the same, nor does it mean everyone is the same. In terms of equity, heterogeneous instruction decreases the likelihood—although it still can exist—that disproportionate numbers of students of color and low-income students will receive a lower quality of instruction. However, good instruction in heterogeneous classes does demand more from teachers: more skill at designing lesson plans and units, more imagination in working with diverse points of views in an organized way, and more freedom to divert from the press to cover a certain amount of material in a finite period of time.

Consequently, the level of resistance to heterogeneous grouping—and a corresponding shift in instruction—may run high among teachers, both because of a sincere belief that differentiated instruction provides best for the differing abilities and interests of students, and because teachers feel ill-prepared to take on such a significant instructional shift. As both researchers and practitioners point out, there is a need for sophisticated professional development for teachers that has a few key components: time for sustained talk and discussion; a somewhat structured, but not scripted, approach to curriculum; the opportunity to field-test new instructional practices, ideally with expert and peer feedback; and ample time to allow new instructional approaches to evolve before assessing their efficacy prematurely.

The quality of leadership figures significantly into the question of whether heterogeneous instruction will be realized or simply acted upon and ultimately dismissed as another educational trend. As each of the practitioners reflects, leadership toward heterogeneity—with a corresponding paradigm shift in instructional practices—needs to be flexible, strong, imaginative, shared, and sure. It is unlikely that a school without a leader who can shelter teachers from political pressure—as well as encourage their best practice—will succeed in shifting its instruction along heterogeneous lines.

It is my intent that this collection of interviews will extend and contribute to the conversation about tracking—and that, in particular, the perspectives of the practitioners included in this volume will help ground some of the theoretical and abstract concepts inherent in educational research. Finally, it is my goal that the reader realize that not all conflicts over the aims and purposes of schooling are hopelessly mired in controversy, without hope of any intelligent action.

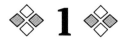

High-Quality
Instruction for All:
Adam Gamoran

Adam Gamoran is Professor of Sociology and Educational Policy Studies at the University of Wisconsin—Madison, where he has been a Principal Investigator for a series of federally funded research centers, including the Center on Organization and Restructuring of Schools (1990–1995), the current Center for Research on Achievement in School Mathematics and Science, and the National Research Center for Improving Achievement in English, both of which began work in the spring of 1996. His research focuses on stratification and inequality in school systems. His most recent publications include a study of ability grouping, teaching, and learning; a study of the achievement benefits of urban magnet schools; and a study of curriculum change and equality of opportunity in Scotland. Gamoran spent 1992–1993 as a Fulbright Scholar at the University of Edinburgh.

To Adam Gamoran, the whole issue of detracking schools and moving to instructional arrangements other than tracks or ability groups could be considered a diversion from the primary issue: the quality of instruction—whatever the structural arrangements for teaching and learning. Political and intense, the current debate over equitable distribution of students, while important, should focus more substantively on the overall quality of instruction, he maintains.

What does high-quality instruction look like? I asked him. How does a parent, for instance, recognize good instruction?

Rather than something that teachers "do" to students, Gamoran asserts that one characteristic of high-quality instruction is the presence of appropriate interaction between teachers and students. "Instruction is what teachers and students do together," he pointed out. "If students are on task when they are in class, complete and hand in their written assignments, those are signs that students are paying attention and are engaged mentally in their work."

But there is a caveat: The presence of on-task behavior and completion of assignments does not mean that high-quality instruction is exemplified by routinized drillwork where compliant students obey the directives of a teacher. Instead, interaction of a particular type signifies high-quality instruction.

Gamoran explained, "When we are identifying high-quality instruction, we look for a lot of interaction between teachers and students as contrasted with situations where students work at their desks, the teacher sits at his or her desk, and they don't talk to each other. We also look for a mix of interaction that focuses on student understanding of the content that is being addressed along with opportunities for students to address that content in a way that is high level, through open-ended questions and questions that require a higher order of thinking, and with discussion that is not superficial but that goes deeply into a single subject. The conversation between students and teachers indicates that teachers take seriously what students have to say; teachers' questions show this. In other words, they are not asking questions simply to check or test students."

He added, "Teachers in these classrooms actually want students to say what is on their minds and they are able to bring their comments into the classroom conversation."

Compliance Versus Interaction

What about parents who might perceive a classroom permeated with lively teacher-student interaction as evidence of poor classroom management or who might yearn for the didactic instruction of their own youth? Gamoran believes that parents who look back nostalgically to a romanticized past of their own schooling experiences need to consider more broadly what their child will learn with this type of instruction.

"Those parents," he said flatly, "have an overly narrow view of what constitutes student learning and what constitutes good teaching. They should want to see their children learn how to solve new problems, figure out complicated situations, talk with other people, and participate as a member of a group. There are a whole range of complicated skills that require students—and people in general—to do much more than work in isolation."

Just as learning to solve new problems and work effectively in groups are new skills that students must acquire, teaching that furthers these skills demands certain innovative techniques and progressive teacher attitudes. How, I asked, can schools support teachers so that they can work to elevate the quality of their instruction?

Appropriate professional development—coupled with adequate planning in the event schools decide to detrack—is a powerful aid to helping teachers improve the quality of their instructional strategies, Gamoran maintains. "It is possible to increase teachers' awareness of the kinds of instructional practices that allow more student participation and more open classroom lessons," he said. "Professional development is one way to help teachers with some concrete strategies to do so, and gain confidence which will help them as they use them.

"Professional development," he continued, "is an important part of the solution and it relates to the tracking issue because there are instances where the administration—school or district—will suddenly decide 'no more tracking.' Without any preparation, teachers will be handed mixed batches of students instead of the tracked groups to which they're accustomed. They will try to use the same instructional practices as before and will find out that they don't work. As a result, they will be very frustrated. Instead of simply mandating detracking schools, school administrators need to work with teachers, providing them opportunities for professional growth so that they'll have better opportunities to prepare and teach students with diverse abilities."

Improving the Quality of Instruction

Given that a system does exist that divides students on the basis of their performance, what can be done to improve the quality of instruction, particularly in lower-ability classes? I inquired.

In his answer, Gamoran referred to the findings of his research. "In one study,[1] I identified low-ability classes in an attempt to find those that were successful. Out of 25 low-ability classes that we studied over a 2-year period, we saw two that we considered successful, in the sense that students kept pace with those in other classes instead of falling further behind. Certain aspects of the relations between teacher and students seemed to be related to the success. Teachers, first of all, held high expectations and refused to give up on the academic curriculum.

"Typically," he enlarged, "teachers in low-track classes believe that teaching academic material is not the main goal for their classes. Instead, they think that the main goal of instruction is to keep their students well-behaved, interested, and achieving at the C level.

"The successful teachers, however, held academic standards for their low-track classes. Second, these teachers worked harder with their low-track classes than with their other classes. Ordinarily, teaching low-track classes is felt to require less work because the material is not as complex. Teachers give out worksheets and kids will stay quiet."

He added, "That is the easy way to get through the day."

But the successful teachers in Gamoran's study refused to take the easy path. "They didn't do that," he stated. "They worked even harder to try to engage their students in conversations and discussion. They checked students, one on one, to make sure they were doing their work. It took extra effort on the part of teachers, and it played out in a lot of question-and-answer and discussion in these classes, more so than what we found in other low-track classes."

An additional dynamic was noticeable in teacher attitudes. "Teachers usually compete with one another to try to teach the top classes," Gamoran pointed out. "The low people on the totem pole, whether it's because of their reputation or their status as new teachers, tend to be assigned to low-track classes. In these schools, the system of assigning weak or inexperienced teachers to low-track classes didn't exist. In fact, in the two cases that I studied, the same teacher taught both a low-track and a high-track class."

Current Sentiments Toward Tracking

Despite the fact that some teachers welcome teaching low-track classes, the majority do not—and although antitracking sentiments are widely publicized, many teachers resist current efforts to detrack schools although they may entertain uneasiness about the equity of the system. The reasons for their objections to teaching only heterogeneous groups can range from a philosophical conviction that tracking and ability grouping provide the best structures to cope with students' diverse abilities as well as a recognition that they are unprepared to teach in other ways.

"If you did a survey of teachers," Gamoran said thoughtfully, "I doubt that you would find that more teachers support detracking over tracking. They don't know how to teach a more diverse group of students, but they feel uneasy about tracking because they see that it is not an equal system."

Since a disproportionate number of minority students are assigned to low-track classes, how can schools combat resegregation? I asked. In his reply, Gamoran emphasized that low-track placement for minority students—although admittedly disproportionate—has less to do with overt prejudice than with low scores on standardized tests.

"The fact is that minority students are overassigned to lower tracks," he responded, "not because there is overt discrimination necessarily but because their test scores are lower. This has the result of producing unequal treatment for minority students since the instruction they receive is not the same across tracks. Advocates for minority students and disadvantaged students are right to argue against tracking, given this situation."

Have desegregation policies made any impact on assignments to tracks? I asked.

"Within desegregated schools," Gamoran observed, "students still are assigned to classes on the basis of test scores. And although it's not true in every case, typically there is no race discrimination over and above test scores differences. Unfortunately, race and test scores are correlated. On the basis of their test scores, kids end up divided on the basis of race as well."

Detracking: Problems and Obstacles

In addition to teachers often possessing a skimpy repertoire of instructional strategies to use with heterogeneous classes, what other problems ensue when schools or districts decide to detrack? I inquired. In his reply, Gamoran referred to the work of Jeannie Oakes, who has identified three problems that occur with detracking: normative, political, and technical.

"The normative problem," he explained, "has to do with the culture in which schools exist. This culture has a widely shared belief that children differ from one another and because they differ, they should be put into different categories. Classes should include kids from a small number of categories, rather than the whole range of categories.

"When we detrack, we create a structure that is inconsistent with the culture. It is very difficult for the participants in the culture to deal with it; it creates a lot of resistance."

The second problem, which is political, means that the interests of certain groups are not realized, Gamoran says. "For example, parents whose children formerly would have been in the high track or honors classes are very concerned about the elimination of those honors classes. Their children would have benefited from those classes and they want them restored."

Teachers frequently share their concern, creating a polarized school climate in which teachers themselves are not detracking advocates. "Teachers who regularly teach honors classes may find it a great burden to have to teach kids suddenly in mixed-ability classes," Gamoran observed. "As a result, they may try to mobilize opinion in favor of the traditional system."

Last is the difficulty teachers experience when they suddenly face mixed-ability classes without appropriate teaching strategies. "This problem has not been solved very well, especially at the secondary level, and particularly for subjects that are seen as sequential, like mathematics. We simply do not have a lot of models of effective teaching for kids in mixed-ability contexts."

Is There a Solution to Tracking?

Is there any solution, given that testing drives the curriculum and determines assignments to tracks? Are there glimmers of hope? I asked.

"I see two solutions to the tracking problem," Gamoran said judiciously. "One is to eliminate it; the other is to maintain it but do a better job with the low-track students. If either of these solutions can succeed, then the test score difference between kids from different racial backgrounds would diminish. Test scores would still make a big difference but they wouldn't promote racial inequality. Beyond that, of course, much of the test score difference has to do with what is going on outside school, not what is occurring inside school."

As he looks to the future of public education, Gamoran insists that he is not pessimistic. "Schools all over the country are exploring ways to increase integration," he said, "not only racial integration but more particularly academic and social integration, integration across academic and economic boundaries in ways that haven't existed before.

"If there is isolation in American schooling," he added, "it's primarily because of isolation in the residences of Americans. Most of the racial isolation in schools is due to the fact that blacks live in racially segregated neighborhoods, not because there is tracking within schools. The real battle for integration in the schools, particularly racial integration, has to be a continuing battle for open housing and for integrated neighborhoods."

He is encouraged by what he sees as movement toward that goal. "Blacks are moving out to suburbs in increasing numbers, particularly in southern cities. Inside schools there is a lot of interest in breaking down barriers, mixing kids from different ability levels, providing a common curriculum, and presenting academic challenges to all kids. However, a great deal of racial isolation remains."

Suburbs, in contrast to cities, have a more pronounced interest in maintaining tracking in schools, he says. "Suburbs are more focused on the top students—and most suburbs don't face problems of race. It is less likely the case in suburban schools that tracking brings resegregation since most of these schools have small numbers of minority students. It's the schools that are integrated, racially or ethnically, that face the greatest challenge from tracking. Tracking in those settings, on average, means resegregation. It's in those schools that we see the greatest incentives for educators who are pursuing goals of equity to dismantle a tracking system."

The Change in Stratification

Are these efforts genuine or is tracking still continuing under another name? I inquired.

"The efforts are very genuine," Gamoran said. "The educators that I read about or meet are very sincere in their attempts to provide more of a common curriculum for all students, but it seems that whenever stratification is eliminated on one side it tends to pop out in some other way."

As an example, he pointed to the research he and his colleagues at the Center on Organization and Restructuring of Schools conducted between 1990 and 1995, in which some schools tried to eliminate ability grouping and tracking by encouraging student choice. "When students choose their courses," Gamoran remarked, "there is a tendency for them to choose courses that are 'appropriate' for their achievement level. This is particularly true in math. In both the high schools and middle schools that we studied, we found strong tendencies for preserving ability grouping in math or preserving the grouping of students according to their performance in math—much more strongly than in other subjects."

He added, "It is hard to know whether that is because there are very rigid ideas about what math is or because there is something in the nature of the subject matter that really makes it necessary to address each child as closely as possible to his or her performance level."

But if students are self-selecting courses, aren't they picking classes where they would be assigned in all likelihood? I asked.

"Definitely, at least in math," Gamoran agreed.

Then some sort of stratification is still occurring, I said, but it is now self-selected rather than assigned. Is that correct?

"Absolutely," Gamoran said. "In subjects other than math, that is less true. The more emphasis there is on integrating across curricular areas, the greater the tendency there is to do so without any kind of leveling. In social studies there is a strong tendency in restructured schools to eliminate ability grouping—to have all students of the same age in the same courses."

While some teachers find that difficult because students have different reading levels, he sees an upbeat attitude toward it in schools that are consciously restructuring themselves. "We did not find the very rigid form of tracking where teachers see the same kids all day because they are the ones in your program, whatever that may be. We are seeing an elimination of that.

"Another trend throughout the country is the tendency to eliminate general track courses considered to be dead-end: basic math and remedial courses that don't lead anywhere."

Even though vocational programs continue, there is a national push toward academic math courses for all students.

Are high school vocational programs as low status as they traditionally have been? I asked.

"In general, yes," Gamoran said carefully, "but there certainly are programs in specific places that are changing that perception. It is very difficult, however, because of the way our society is structured. If you go into a job that requires a college education you have higher status than if you enter a job that doesn't require a college education. The preparatory programs are stratified correspondingly."

Yet he sees a solution: integrating academic and vocational education for all students. "One student might have a greater emphasis on vocational education, and another student might have a greater emphasis on academic material, but there would be an integration of academic or vocational education in everybody's program. This may help to mitigate this problem."

While Gamoran sees this integration as a promising move toward a common curriculum, he painstakingly differentiates between a common and a national curriculum. "A common curriculum could be a common curriculum for all students in the district, or it could be statewide, or it could be national, although I don't believe a national curriculum will happen in the United States. There are possibilities for state-level curricular policies that could be much stronger than they are currently. Most importantly, that would have some kind of testing to go along with it."

He calls discussion of a national, statewide, or districted curriculum "pointless" unless it is accompanied by hard discussion and thought about testing that will accompany it. "Some people are very much afraid of testing because they believe we will end up with teachers teaching to the test, and they say that very pejoratively. My argument is that it depends on whether the tests are good. If they are, then teaching to the test is a good thing."

Good tests would be those that are challenging, Gamoran says, "that raise expectations, that allow students chances to succeed, and also provide incentives for students to try their hardest to learn whatever subject matter they are trying to master. There are some reasons to think that the national test or a state test is desirable and to make that work, we are talking about a common curriculum."

A common curriculum—and an accompanying scheme of assessment—does not mean that public schools are sliding inexorably toward privatization, he believes. "Private school choice would have very negative effects. Most people realize this. Political circumstances will prevent that from happening."

However, Gamoran eschews a prescriptive stance toward tracking and ability grouping. "Each school needs to take a hard look at what it does and should consider eliminating or reducing its ability grouping program. That should be a decision of conscience. Where it is eliminated, the schools should provide opportunities for teachers to learn to teach students in different kinds of classrooms. Where they don't eliminate ability grouping, they should definitely help teachers, particularly those who teach low-ability students, in ways that provide high-quality academic experiences for those students.

"I don't think," he emphasized, "that all schools should come to the same conclusion."

In those cases where schools decide not to eliminate ability grouping or tracking, what rationale can they offer to their critics? I inquired.

"They can respond that the nature of the subject matter is such that it is not feasible to provide instruction to a widely diverse group of students all in the same classroom. Many educators believe that a better mechanism to maximize the potential of each student is to divide the students according to their performance level, provide all of them with instruction that is of high quality and coming from enthusiastic teachers who are well prepared, and as part of a sequence that leads somewhere rather than to a dead end. If that could be done for all students, then students would be better off than they are now."

Note

1. See Gamoran, A., Nystrand, M., Berends, M., & LePore, P. C. (1995). An organizational analysis of the effects of ability grouping. *American Educational Research Journal, 32*(4), 687-715.

2

Tracking and American Culture: Reba Neukom Page

Reba Neukom Page studies and teaches about curriculum, interpretive research methodology, and sociocultural foundations of education at Harvard University, where she is a Visiting Associate Professor of Education, and at the University of California, Riverside, where she is an Associate Professor. Page's interests developed during the 10 years she taught high school English, history and social studies, and special education and are expressed in several articles and two books: Lower-Track Classrooms: A Curricular and Cultural Perspective *and (coedited with Linda Valli)* Curriculum Differentiation: Interpretive Studies in U.S. Secondary Schools.

A profound paradox encircles the ongoing debate about differentiation of the curriculum in the United States—one that means that curriculum differentiation and its offspring, such as tracking and ability grouping, cannot be considered intelligently without taking American culture into account. This is Reba Neukom Page's most particular point: that in order to penetrate the swirl of acrimonious debate about tracking, it is necessary to understand that tracking practices reflect fundamental tensions and polarities within American culture.

Under what circumstances, I asked her, is it appropriate to differentiate the curriculum? Are there circumstances when it is clearly inappropriate?

Page said in reply, "Every teacher and every school encounters this question: Should we teach different kinds of knowledge to different types of students? Usually people who say 'yes' argue that kids have different talents, interests, and ambitions. We want to honor those differences, and we think that differentiating knowledge is necessary if we want to be fair—and also if we want to have excellent education. We say that we can't push everybody into one pigeonhole and expect that they will all blossom."

That argument seems straightforward, she says, until one carefully examines both quantitative and qualitative data on tracking. "The modal pattern seems to be that kids in lower-track classes tend to be from lower-class families. In lower-track classes, they often are exposed to lower-track or lower-status knowledge. Critics argue that this then prepares them for lower-class futures. So, rather than honoring the differences that exist between people, critics contend that through curriculum differentiation we are simply reproducing an inequitable social order and violating our ideals of equality."

An additional layer of complexity stems from the research on tracking and ability grouping, which contains persistently conflicting findings, she points out. "One very interesting article[1] shows that on almost any aspect of tracking, whether it is achievement or self-esteem or whatever, the research evidence is mixed." In the absence of clear research findings that weigh on one side of the debate or the other, answers to whether or not schools should differentiate the curriculum depend, Page says, "on who someone is reading."

Clearly, this does not guide the well-intentioned practitioner who seeks a definitive answer to the question posed about providing different knowledge for different students. But seeking a definitive answer, true for all times and all places, may be the problem. Page maintains that some clarity can be gained if one steps away from the arguments themselves to see the pattern of tracking talk: a pattern of polarized opinions clustered at the extremes with little in the middle.

"In debates about tracking, we consistently and repeatedly construct differentiated curriculum as either good or bad, clearly one way or the other," she pointed out. "Critics of tracking dismiss the arguments of tracking's proponents. Proponents don't consider the evidence offered by critics. As a result, rather than experiencing some sort of serious sustained engagement over complex issues, we end up with a polarized and often simplistic casting of the issues—which results in what some people call the tracking wars—a stalemate which, ironically, maintains the status quo."

She noted, "The more we argue about tracking in this way, the more we end up having it but not owning up to having it, not understanding why we do, and not studying the consequences of having it."

Curriculum Differentiation and American Culture

This polarity and tension is reflected in policy proposals, Page maintains, that demand both standardization and individualization of curriculum, and school practices that reveal the presence of tracking although school staff most frequently do not acknowledge its presence. "One way to understand this duality," she observed, "is to think of curriculum differentiation as a cultural practice. The culture in the United States is one that is oriented around equally cherished but contradictory values of individualism, on the one hand, and the common good on the other.

"Our history and our institutions reflect our continuing oscillation between those values," she continued. "It may seem obvious that differentiating the curriculum satisfies our commitment to individualism. But we need to realize too that when a group is differentiated, we simultaneously *create* a group by putting people together.

"My argument is that the practice of differentiating curriculum, say through tracking students, persists in part because it reflects and re-creates *both* of these core values: individualism *and* the common good—and not just one of them or the other."

The paradox is especially pronounced in programs such as women's studies or black studies, she believes. "In such programs, we find it perfectly legitimate and even praiseworthy to set people apart on the basis of race or gender. We can argue that these courses are needed and will have positive outcomes for solidarity among group members as well as for excellence in education. We don't see tracking, however, in quite those terms.

"For example, at one high school I studied, being in a lower-track class was very stigmatizing—just as critics of tracking would predict. At a second high school, however, tracking was seen by students as a smart 'con' of a relatively unimportant process of schooling. Kids chose to be in lower-track classes to get through school in as easy a way as possible. It's hard for us, as educators, to think that not everyone sees going to school as beneficial."

Given how deeply rooted these conflicting yet equally honored values are in American culture, I asked Page: How likely is it that tracking can be abolished and replaced with a reconceptualized curriculum that honors differences yet believes that students should learn together and can gain from divergent points of view?

"Cultures are social institutions," Page replied contemplatively. "If they're constructed, they can be reconstructed. I'm not arguing that schools are stuck with tracking forever and can't do anything about it, but I also have enough training with anthropologists as opposed to some organizational theorists to think that school cultures are very resistant to change and are very hard to change. I'm not optimistic about 1-day inservices for teachers producing miraculous results, nor am I optimistic that pronouncements from superintendents will have much measurable effect."

She added, "These notions of changing school cultures quickly are misguided at best. My sense is that to even vaguely think that we might do something about these matters will require a massive investment of resources."

On the positive side, a contradictory culture can prompt some interesting inventions, she argues, and showcase some of the best the nation has to offer. "We have a bicameral form of government that recognizes majority rule *and* protects minority rights," she observed. "We have a House of Representatives where states are represented by their population *and* a Senate in which, no matter how large the state, each gets two votes.

"We can think that a contradictory culture is generative when we're smart and lucky about it, and stalemated when we're not so thoughtful. In other words, we ought to be able to accomplish something about these issues but we have to be very clear about the complexity of what we are trying to undertake."

It is tempting, I suggested, although misguided, to believe that a decision about tracking and curriculum differentiation—one way or the other—will constitute some sort of magic bullet that will eradicate past errors and quickly transform schooling.

"It's worrisome," Page agreed, "that the number of magic bullets seem to come at us faster and faster. More frequently than earlier in the century we have a new crisis of some kind in education every time we turn around. The public gets worried and expects experts to work to find the solution to the crisis. Lo and behold, the solution is found but very shortly we find it didn't work—and then the next 'crisis' is on the doorstep. This cycle of crisis, reform, failed reform, next crisis, is something that the political scientist Murray Edelman writes about a lot. He says the cycle benefits elites because, when the public is worried, it hands over resources with the assurance that the crisis will be taken care of.

"Edelman's work leads me to think that as these crises come faster and faster, especially since World War II, that they begin to accumulate and, in a sense, undermine any confidence we have that we can do anything about our social problems. In other words, we may have thought at one time that someone was in charge and could do something about a crisis. But as failed reforms accumulate faster and faster, classroom teachers and taxpayers begin to say: 'The machine is broken.' We become disillusioned with our social institutions, and especially with public education.

"School reformers often dismiss high school teachers who criticize the latest reform proposal by saying, 'We tried that before and it didn't work.' Maybe those teachers aren't just being stubborn. Maybe school reformers should take their comments about the *history* of school reform seriously and look at the demoralization that can accompany the constant push to change and innovate."

When a Differentiated Curriculum Makes Sense

Are there circumstances that demand a differentiated curriculum? I inquired. Is it ever the best course of action, or do the costs clearly outweigh the benefits?

"Some research suggests it is appropriate under some circumstances," Page said, "particularly the curriculum studies that argue that the knowledge schools teach has to be congruent with children's cultures. In these studies, researchers found that when the discourse in reading groups, for example, was similar to the talk that children experienced at home and in their communities, reading achievement went up. As a result, they argued for a differentiated curriculum in reading so that children felt comfortable with the talk in the classroom. In a similar vein, some people suggest that the curriculum offered to poor children, for example, should in some way resonate with or be relevant to the way they see the world."

Yet, Page says, this argument does not appear to have much influence on the debate over tracking—"the most prevalent form of curriculum differentiation, at least in American secondary schools," she noted. "The logic of the argument is that it is all right to differentiate curriculum on the basis of cultural difference but not on the basis of academic or intellectual difference. But if adolescents can't read well, there's no point in giving them Shakespeare just because it's 'high-status knowledge.' And there's no point in handing them drill-and-practice worksheets in phonics either. Tracking debates run roughshod over the particular complexities of teaching and learning in classrooms."

The argument rolls on to encompass unisex schools and classrooms. "Some feminists advocate gender-differentiated classes and presumably gender-differentiated curriculum, because the presence of boys in math and science classrooms makes a difference for girls' achievement."

Is this inappropriate? To Page, the inappropriateness of differentiated curriculum can be seen in its potential for immutability. "If students are locked in forever, it seems inappropriate. Also, if there are consequences for track placement, it is inappropriate. One example would be if you couldn't go to college because you took certain courses."

Heated Rhetoric, Angry Debate

The rhetoric that surrounds the tracking and ability grouping issue, I said, seems especially acrimonious. Why does this topic bring out such extreme emotions on both sides? I asked.

"There is a history associated with this topic," Page said, "and always this kind of shouting match surrounding it. One reason could be that we don't see the extent to which we value *both* individualism and the common good. Instead, we talk solely in terms of their opposition and then we polarize. It's not surprising, because seeing that America has a paradoxical culture isn't what most of us see. When we encounter an issue like tracking, we tend to be on one side or the other.

"Yet," she added, "if we can begin to see that even if we're critical of tracking, we still value individualism, and that even if someone supports tracking, they are not insensitive to issues of equality, we may be able to see that there is more common ground in this dichotomous argument than the dichotomous way of arguing would suggest.

"In other words, if America *is* a paradoxical culture, then presumably the advocates of tracking and the critics of tracking would both value the common good *and* individualism. It isn't an 'either-or' proposition. Thinking that, we fall into a polarized discourse that ends up as a shouting match. The shouting match just maintains things as they are."

Another reason for the acrimonious quality the debate has assumed could be the amount of time devoted to careful discussion of it, she proposes. "We don't devote much time to it, so once we get together, we have to get through things with sound bites and slogans. The discussion also often focuses strictly on grouping. But grouping is not the problem. Curriculum and instruction is the problem. Whether students are grouping or not we have to ask: What should schools teach, and why?"

Focusing on the structural arrangements through which instruction occurs, rather than on what knowledge is taught and in what way, is a fundamental mistake, Page believes. "Grouping is easy to think about in a sense," she enlarged. "Do we do it or don't we? But once you open up curriculum and teaching, the question becomes: What we are going to teach, and why? We have been un-willing to devote the resources that are needed if we are going to address that question seriously. And in a sense, tracking is a sort of red herring, diverting us away from those issues. We assume that once we remove tracks and put all children together in a classroom, the problems of inequality and individualism are solved."

The fact that many schools claim they "do" heterogeneous grouping but in fact continue to differentiate instruction supports Page's contention. "Most recently in California, the state has rec-ommended that schools do away with the old layer-cake curricu-lum in high school science: a year of biology, a year of physics, and a year of chemistry. Instead, the state recommended replacing that with heterogeneously grouped classes in what is called integrated science. Integrated science is a science curriculum for all students in which all the sciences are brought to bear on certain broad prac-tical themes, such as evolution, the universe, and so forth."

Page's research in selected high schools in Southern California has enabled her to watch the process through which schools have tried to implement this recommendation. "In these high schools, ninth graders typically took general science, biology, or honors bi-ology. There was a section or two of sheltered and special educa-tion general science too. The reform was: All ninth graders in integrated sciences."

She continued, "The high schools I have studied discontinued the general science courses which used to be for kids who were not as good at science or not as interested in it or who didn't want to devote as much effort to it. They were supposed to discontinue ninth-grade biology as well. But when the school board met to an-nounce this and discuss it, parents appeared at the meeting and there was a loud outcry against heterogeneously grouped inte-grated science instead of biology.

"No one that I know of argued for general science, but they did argue for ninth-grade biology. The decision of the board was inter-esting. It decided that in general most ninth graders would enroll in this new integrated science course and would be heterogene-ously grouped *except* when students requested individually to be placed in biology. If you think about it, who are the students who are going to *request* biology? When you consider this, you realize that the schools could end up more stratified than they were before. In addition, the schools did not do away with honors biology and they didn't do away with special education science. The following year, they reintroduced differentiation within the heterogeneously grouped integrated sciences: There were sections of 'embedded honors integrated science.' On top of it all, the curriculum in the integrated sciences is a kind of hodgepodge of subjects, with an emphasis on biology."

So what they managed to accomplish, Page observes, is "put old wine in old bottles but with a new label. In the course of 1 year, general science has gone. In the second year, biology sections were halved. But the teachers were given almost no resources to develop an integrated curriculum. If it had happened, there *would* have been a revolution in the science curriculum. Imagine going from teaching standard biology to teaching integrated science, in which you teach not only biology but chemistry, physics, and earth science, all around these thematic units. The resources provided to the teacher who, at each school, piloted the first integrated science course consisted of 3 or 4 days of release time."

She sums up the attempt at curriculum reform: "Not surprisingly, the revolution has not happened."

The Need for Resources

What sorts of things should schools consider carefully, I asked, when they believe they want to move to heterogeneous instruction? What do they need to discuss? What needs to be in place for the change to succeed? What kinds of resources need to be committed to the effort?

"The thing that isn't there," Page said, "is time. It takes time to do any of this. Particularly, it takes time for sustained talk about these matters. Sometimes we think that talking is sitting around, avoiding action or the problem. But from another perspective, talking *is* action. It's the way we find out exactly what the problem is so that we can then think well about what we want to do differently."

Typically, decisions around tracking are made in a top-down fashion, she says, in what she terms "a hierarchy of command.

Someone says the school is or isn't going to differentiate curriculum; other people tell the people below them that that is what is going to happen. Those people pass it on to the people below them. In that hierarchy, there is no room for any sustained conversation about what the proposed change is; what, precisely, will be different or better; and whether or not it's a good idea. There is no room or time for the complexity of curriculum change."

Instead, she sees effective curriculum development as a community enterprise involving teachers, parents, school board members, and students in a conversation about when, where, and for what purposes they might differentiate the curriculum or not. "These are *local* questions," she emphasized. "They are particular questions. Not paying attention to the specific contexts in which tracking occurs leads us back to the all-or-nothing answers that tracking is always good or always bad. It leads us away from the complex particulars of real classrooms. It also leads us away from taking responsibility ourselves for our practices—all too often schools track or detrack because 'research' tells them to, not because they have thought carefully about what they are doing.

"That, in and of itself, would be a remarkable change in the way schools operate. But given that people are thinking in terms of fewer resources for schools rather than more, I am very pessimistic about any serious change in the curriculum."

Truly Heterogeneous Instruction

If parents and school staff can experience the value of a curriculum change, the change will be expedited, Page believes. "That entails not just selling the change," she cautions, "in a spin-control sort of way, but literally thinking about how one engages parents and students in the advantages and complexity of what is proposed. It may be that schools want to think out where they want to try to do heterogeneous grouping, both strategically and tactically. For example, it may be easier to do in some kinds of experiences than in others."

Although heterogeneous grouping is usually attempted in the academic subjects, she refers to the work of James Conant in the

1950s in which he viewed classes such as physical education and homeroom as places where students could be brought together from diverse backgrounds and abilities. "Perhaps schools need to contemplate the kinds of experiences other than academic classes in which to allow students and their parents to see the value of coming into contact with people who are not quite so similar."

If schools decide to embark upon heterogeneous grouping, how can they ensure that their assignments to groups are truly heterogeneous? I asked.

"Educators, like all of us," Page replied, "perceive people according to cultural categories, so they may not be the people to make the assignments. Sometimes as we try to achieve heterogeneity, we reinscribe differentiation, by paying attention to differences of race, ability, or whatever as we try to arrange a heterogeneous group. It's a type of Catch-22 in a way."

Random assignments could be used to achieve heterogeneity, Page says. "But schools probably would be very unwilling to do that because they would be unsure of what they would get. There again is this tight play between individualizing and equalizing. We expect schools to differentiate. They must pay attention to difference; they are un-American if they don't honor the integrity of each individual. And at the same time, we tell them not to discriminate."

But the difference between differentiation and discrimination is hard to ascertain, she points out. "That is what we see when schools try to construct heterogeneous groups. The heterogeneous group often embodies the key principles of differentiation that the school supposedly is moving away from. That's part of the paradox of the culture."

Raising the Quality of Instruction Overall

How realistic, I asked, is it to plan to raise the quality of instruction in low-track classes—without a move away from differentiation to heterogeneity?

"What we have proposed as a curriculum for so-called average and below-average kids has never been thought out very well," Page reflected. "Thinking about curriculum and doing a better job with it are things for which schools can be responsible. Schools can't do anything about the social classes from which kids come to them, but they can do something about the lessons they offer.

"That is a responsibility," she added, "that schools have not accepted very well. We focus on the politics of identity—who kids are—and then we assume we can simply derive the knowledge they should be taught from that. What we need instead is some serious attention to curriculum itself. However, the important coda to that is that the curriculum is not the answer for all problems. Sometimes when we talk about being responsible for curriculum and all the good things that the curriculum can solve, we neglect the fact that curriculum has quite limited effects. At best, its effects are limited."

If thoughtful people—educators and citizens alike—can remember that scholastic problems are also social problems, the discussion that follows can be the most productive, she contends. "We educators shouldn't pass the buck and say: 'Schools can't do anything differently.' We should be conscious, however, of the modest effects that schools will have. That's extremely important, not just so that we don't become discouraged, but also so that we don't become too full of pride or hubris."

Note

1. See Gamoran, A., & Berends, M. (1987). The effects of stratification in secondary schools: Synthesis of survey and ethnographic research. *Review of Educational Research, 57,* 415-435.

3

Advocating for Inclusive Instruction: Anne Wheelock

Anne Wheelock's interest in school reform and advocacy for students took root in 1968, when she directed a neighborhood tutoring program in Boston and observed that many otherwise competent children failed to succeed in the Boston public schools. As part of that experience, she also worked with parents whose children with disabilities were excluded from or isolated within public schools. From 1981 to 1992 she directed community education programs on public policy issues and children's rights at the Massachusetts Advocacy Center. While at the Center, she also authored several reports on middle school reform, dropout prevention, and school tracking and placement practices. She is the author of Crossing the Tracks: How "Untracking" Can Save America's Schools *(New York: New Press, 1992), which describes alternatives to tracking and ability grouping and details the steps schools take to offer a high-quality education to all students in multiability groups. Wheelock works as a writer on school reform for the Edna McConnell Clark Foundation and has published several articles and reports on the promise and process of "untracking" and school reform.*

What Anne Wheelock describes as "one of the most shocking experiences I ever had" led to her work as an advocate for detracking schools—out of her conviction that through multiability instruction, all children will have equal access to important knowledge and an equal opportunity to learn.

Wheelock still remembers her moment of epiphany, which occurred while she was working for the Massachusetts Advocacy Center, analyzing data from the Boston public schools. The data, she reports, described middle and high school course enrollment in math and science. "First," she recalled, "we found that there were only tiny numbers of ninth graders enrolled in algebra. In one of the schools, only 2.9% of the ninth graders were enrolled in algebra. The high—meaning the most students at any school enrolled in algebra—was only 50%. The average was about 25%."

Her next discovery galvanized her: Only one Latino student out of the entire Boston public schools was enrolled in calculus. "It absolutely bowled me over," she said, remembering how astonished she was at the time. "That was the motivation for me to look for alternatives. I knew that we had to find schools who had recognized problems related to tracking and ability grouping, who had realized that these practices held kids back from learning."

From "Untracking" to Heterogeneous Instruction

How, I asked, did you decide to use the word *untracking* to describe the move away from tracking and ability grouping to heterogeneous instruction? Is there any significance to choosing the word *untracking* over *detracking*?

"I tried to find a word that would communicate a process," Wheelock replied. "I understand that people are trying to make a distinction between detracking and untracking, but there is none as far as I'm concerned. Untracking, to me, communicates the process of change, specifically encompassing three aspects of a process."

The three aspects, she says, include replacing ability-grouped and homogeneous classes with multiability classes, providing access to a strong curriculum within heterogeneous classes, and taking steps to signal that high expectations—formerly reserved for top-track students—will be extended to all students. "That was my definition of untracking when I began," she added.

What would aid educators and the general public the most in changing long-held views about the usefulness or even the imperative of tracking and ability grouping? I inquired.

"Some educators might say it was a combination of professional development and teacher advocates in their schools who kept prodding everyone along," Wheelock observed. "But ultimately what reaches people is actually seeing students who have been dismissed as average or not up to real challenges actually learn and produce acceptable, if not exceptional, work.

"I don't think anybody claims that students suddenly produce exemplary, dazzling work, but it is very convincing to see students produce acceptable work at a much higher standard than previously."

She added, "There is no formula, of course. So much depends on the community. It helps enormously to have a constituency of parents and a community that supports multiability grouping, or to be in a community in which there is an absence of parents who really refuse to support this.

"It also helps to have the leadership in the schools set the tone for a different kind of learning, giving teachers the responsibility and authority to make decisions about how they are going to introduce a higher content of curriculum into the classroom."

However, how one succeeds in changing long-held beliefs about the nature of intelligence is more complicated, she acknowledges. "That is something that unsettles a lot of us," she noted wearily.

Philosophies about human intelligence and capacity to learn vary widely, Wheelock points out, from the convictions of those she terms "true believers"—teachers and other school staff fundamentally committed to the notion that all students can produce high-quality work—to others who adamantly disagree. "The teachers who believe in untracking have a passion for children, a passion for their subject, and a passion for democracy. If schools want to untrack, it certainly helps to have a core group of teachers who find it intolerable to separate kids."

The Role of Professional
Development in Untracking

Many people point to the need for professional development, I said to Wheelock, without a great deal of elaboration about what it needs to encompass in order to be effective. I asked her: What factors need to be present in professional development so that teachers have some structure and guidelines in order to ensure that their instruction—and curriculum—will be appropriate for heterogeneous classes?

There are many types of professional development available, Wheelock said, ranging from the purely motivational to the rigidly prescriptive—with a great deal in between. "Unfortunately, a good deal of professional development still does not get teachers to look at the content of their curriculum, which is critical," she said. "Professional development that seems to work is organized around curriculum, including specific curriculum content, and around specific curriculum packages that teachers can implement as a team in their schools. The more time I spend in schools, the more I think that teachers need some very powerful curriculum packages or teaching strategies. Examples might be the Connected Mathematics Project or the Interactive Mathematics Program."

Powerful professional development cannot rely solely on the purely motivational, although it may have a limited value, Wheelock believes. Instead, having a framework that guides curriculum can keep teachers from floundering and, ultimately, not making any changes due to a lack of structure.

"It's a little easier to work from a curriculum than it is to get a handle on the more generic cooperative learning strategies," she noted. "The Integrated Mathematics Project, for instance, is designed for heterogeneous classes. The professional development it offers is exemplary because it offers extended time in the summer, designed for teams of mathematics teachers from different schools."

The importance of an extended period of time for professional development cannot be overestimated, she maintains. Truly effective professional development includes a feedback loop that provides teachers the opportunity to be observed and receive constructive evaluation of their practice once they return to their classrooms.

"In this particular curriculum, follow-up visits continue during the school year," Wheelock pointed out, "so that the trainers can observe teachers in their classroom. The curriculum includes new teaching strategies, like cooperative learning, group work, and Socratic questioning, and is tied to real curriculum activities so that teachers don't have to invent the curriculum from scratch."

Isn't there a fine line, I inquired, between the guidance certain curriculum packages can offer and the stultifying effect of a rigid, "canned" program?

"Yes," Wheelock agreed, "this is not scripted. It does provide some structure, some goals, and it's *standards*-based, which helps prevent mediocre content from watering down the curriculum."

This program, along with other exemplary curriculum packages, includes what Wheelock lists as the elements for exemplary professional development: extended time for in-depth conversations among teachers, continuing opportunities for teachers to network and talk about what they're doing in relation to real pieces of student work, and a heavy focus on content. "Increasingly, if we want teachers to teach writing, higher-order thinking, Socratic questioning, and the deeper concepts of mathematics, science, history, and literature, they have to have these experiences as well."

In other words, it is necessary for professional development to provide the same opportunities to teachers that we want for students, she emphasizes. "How else," she asked, "can students learn from their teachers?"

Structural Change as Diversion From Real Reform

To what extent, I asked, do you see attention devoted to structural changes—changing from tracking and ability grouping to heterogeneous grouping might be an example—as diversionary from significant change within a school? Is there a probability, as Fred Newmann has observed (Lockwood, in press), that teachers can polarize around their positions, either pro or con, and end up forgetting its original purpose?

"I agree," Wheelock said strongly, "and add this: What I've observed is that the structural changes can become ends in and of themselves."

Enlarging upon her point, she added, "For the untracking schools that I found, untracking was seen as a means to an end: improved learning for all students—and I really mean all students, including top-track students. It's also necessary to realize that the energy that goes into taking sides can be enormously draining."

Her observations in schools support her belief that significant change does not occur because one side of an issue wins over another. "The move toward multiability grouping, which offers access to valued knowledge for all kids, is not decided on the basis of one position being stronger than another. Rather, it's decided on the basis of whether a school can actually show some gains or really demonstrate that this kind of learning is richer, more interesting, and eventually results in higher achievement.

"It really is," she added thoughtfully, "one of these 'you have to see it to believe it' kinds of changes."

A definite contributing factor to the possibility that school staff can become frozen in adversarial and polarized positions around a change can be a leadership vacuum. "In the absence of strong leadership," Wheelock said, "a school's community is further polarized—and it freezes the school for further change."

Mired in acrimony? I asked.

"Sometimes," Wheelock said judiciously, "or it takes different forms. For example, I know a high school in Massachusetts where the English teachers have taken it on themselves to improve their curriculum and group kids heterogeneously. They have not had the proactive support of either the administration or of other teachers, for the most part.

"This has made it very difficult for them to sustain this change, one year to the next, to deal with the impact of scheduling and the fact that they're not in a school where the norm is to expect high-quality work from all kids. So they always are bucking the culture of the school. They're trying to introduce change, but they're really going against the grain."

This constant tension—combined with real philosophical differences between the English teachers and the rest of the school—

has had an oppressive, inhibiting effect on their efforts. "This means that they also are out on a limb without support, which means that parents can come in and abuse them at will. If a parent decides to do this, there is no principal or superintendent present who can defend their practice on the basis of research or on the basis of data that is being gathered schoolwide."

She noted darkly, "Soon these teachers aren't going to be able to sustain their efforts."

Solutions to Tracking

I was curious to discover how Wheelock would react to Adam Gamoran's two solutions to the tracking issue: either detrack schools or focus on improving instruction in the low tracks. Does one recommendation seem more practical than another? Since Wheelock is a determined and passionate advocate for detracking schools, her response surprised me.

"The latter, focusing on improving instruction in low tracks, is certainly a reasonable beginning," she stated. "It all depends on where you start. If you start in a suburban high school and the low track means that the kids are still performing at the 50th percentile, you can get quite a lot of mileage out of just improving the curriculum and instruction offered in the low tracks."

Data from New York City support that contention, she added. "In ninth-grade math in New York City, there are at least two levels. There are the courses in which they are preparing to take the statewide exam: the Regents. And there are courses that are very low-level and do not prepare the kids to take the statewide Regents exam.

"With some 60% of ninth graders enrolled in the Regents-level course, 37% were failing. Then a mandate came down that required all ninth graders to enroll in Regents-level math, boosting enrollment in Regents math in ninth grade to 90%. Forty-two percent of those kids failed—but even though a higher percentage of kids were failing, a much larger group had access to Regents-level math, which they had never taken before, and in terms of raw numbers, thousands more succeeded.

"Just giving them access to better curriculum," she pondered, "resulted in a huge improvement in the numbers of kids who were exposed to higher-content knowledge and who succeeded in the improved curriculum."

What about the commonly held assumptions that high-track instruction is uniformly good, of high quality—and if only students could receive the type of instruction offered in high-track classes, their opportunities to learn and succeed would be dramatically increased? I asked. Research does not support that belief, and yet it is quite prevalent.

"Sometimes," Wheelock said slowly, "high-track instruction is very ordinary and traditional. The teacher talks; the students sit in their seats and take notes. They look just like college classes and so people think that this is high-content instruction. Whether kids are learning or not is a separate issue.

"It's not necessarily teaching for understanding," she added dryly.

Limitations to Improving Low-Track Instruction

Although improving instruction in low tracks can have its advantages as a strategic starting point for change, it has drawbacks as well, Wheelock pointed out. "It will have a limited payoff. At some point, real learning for understanding also benefits from having divergent thinking and different viewpoints expressed. Socratic discussions, for example, really benefit from students taking a look at a common text but reading and interpreting it from their own points of view. Projects that involve complex thinking and are meant to engage kids in real-world work benefit from the work of groups of kids who have different talents, abilities, and perspectives."

At the secondary level in particular, Wheelock continued, some problems in low-track classes that have accumulated over the years of low-track placement—and lower-status knowledge offered in low tracks—are virtually insoluble, no matter how dedicated the teacher. "By the time many low-track students get to 8th, 9th, or 10th grade, their classes are full of kids who are 2 years over age for grade. They're the 15-year-olds who are in the 8th grade and have outgrown their desks. Even the best curriculum and instruction can only take you so far under those circumstances."

When Extra Help Is Needed

What happens, I asked, when teachers at the middle and high school levels may feel a philosophical commitment to detracking, but can't imagine teaching heterogeneously when many of their low-track students haven't learned to read?

"There are steps that schools have to take," Wheelock responded, "to get those kids extra help, the kind of help that allows them to succeed in a multiability classroom. That means that some grouping will still occur. In the schools that I found contending with this issue, they were still offering some powerful instruction in separate classes in addition to their heterogeneous classes. They were using specific programs, but they were putting kids into separate groups to jump-start them in reading."

One school she observed offered thematic instruction. "They had separate classes for kids who were scoring below the 30th percentile in reading. In these classes, they would be introduced to a unit on survival, for instance, and their anchor book would be *Lord of the Flies*. Prior to that unit, they would pull the kids out and show them the video of *Lord of the Flies*, introduce them to the main characters, and talk about the character and plot. That would happen 2 weeks before they were going to work on the unit with the rest of the class. This sort of extra help jump-started them for the classwork that would come later."

And there was no stigma attached to those students because of the extra help they received? I probed.

"No, not at all," Wheelock replied. Apparently, teachers were able to provide extra help and maintain the integrity of heterogeneous instruction without an additional stigma attached to those students who were the recipients of the additional aid.

Rather than being too concerned about possible negative effects that may accrue if students are targeted for special help—and yet left in heterogeneous classes—Wheelock expresses concern that too many schools end up determined to treat all students exactly the same. Clearly, she does not agree with that philosophy.

"A lot of schools that are either untracking or thinking about untracking almost go overboard to treat kids the same," she commented, "and that's a misapplication of the principles of equity.

"Untracking," she emphasized, "does *not* require that you treat all kids the same. Untracking requires that you get kids the resources they need so that they can succeed in a heterogeneous high-content classroom. Sometimes, that means different resources for different kids, extra time for some kids, Saturday classes for some kids, or double-dose classes for some kids."

Rather than steering their course away from providing some differentiated instruction in special formats, Wheelock believes that the task before teachers of multiability classrooms is to make them safe places where everyone can succeed—and simultaneously risk failure. "All kids benefit from that," she pointed out.

"As an example, I observed an eighth-grade high-track class in a university town where the kids had been studying Greek myths. One girl suddenly exclaimed, 'You mean Mount Olympus is a real place?' Some of the kids turned on her and said, 'You are so stupid! You shouldn't be in this class.' "

That experience, she observes, supports the notion that a different kind of learning climate is essential, one that, as she explains, "has no costs associated with asking questions and the feeling that you don't know something. Everybody has questions! Teachers have to understand that the real costs of learning occur when students feel that they can't ask questions, that they can't reveal that they don't know something.

"This often happens in top-track classes," she added sadly, "whether it's because the kids feel they'll be knocked down into a lower track or they'll be seen to be stupid and they're not allowed to appear stupid."

Making classrooms safe for extremely bright students is another goal of heterogeneous instruction, Wheelock added—a point often overlooked. "There are students, particularly minority students or poor kids, who have been put in a position in tracked schools where they have to choose between educational opportunity and peer acceptance. If you walk through supposedly integrated schools, you often see top-track classes in which there are one or two African American or Latino kids.

"These kids are in a terrible position. It is not safe for them to be smart because the adults are saying, 'If you want to get benefits for being smart, we're going to segregate you from your peers.' As a result, many kids choose not be smart."

Creating a "safe" learning environment for exceptional students is a reasonable goal that can be achieved, she argues. "I've seen a kinder learning atmosphere in some of the Socratic seminars in Padeia schools, where there are students with very different backgrounds. These students sit together, examine a text, and talk about that text from different viewpoints. I have seen students listening to each other carefully, paraphrasing one another, acknowledging an agreement or a disagreement in a way that would put some adult groups to shame."

Duality and Paradox Related to Tracking: Resolving Conflicting Values

How, I asked, do you see conflicting values playing out in the debate about tracking and ability grouping? How might the debate be resolved?

"I see considerable duality," Wheelock responded thoughtfully. "We value equal opportunity, and we also value merit. On the one hand, we try to act on the notion that all students are entitled to equal access to knowledge, schooling, and the opportunity to learn. On the other hand, we really do operate on some assumptions that some students are more deserving than others.

"Part of the latter beliefs mean that a young person really has to prove herself as a learner in order to be placed so that she will have the opportunity to learn—or her parents have to prove themselves."

This duality is reflected in data that reveal that race has considerable impact on track placement. "In one desegregation case," Wheelock continued, "the district looked at the test scores of students who were in different track levels. They found that Asian students with the exact same scores were 10 times more likely than

Latino kids to be placed in the top groups. White students were 7 times more likely than Latino kids with the same test scores to be placed in the top groups.

"The district asked: 'Why?' And the teachers responded, 'Those students have parents who really push them, who will make sure that they do their homework.' There was an undercurrent of beliefs that some kids are more deserving than others, regardless of their purported ability. It is very intriguing that this whole issue around grouping, access to knowledge, and expectations for what students can do becomes the arena in which the tension between these dualities plays itself out."

Wheelock devotes considerable thought to this subject, and to her own role as an advocate for detracking schools. "If I step out of an advocacy role," she concluded evenly, "where I have my own passions and beliefs, and just look at the situation with a more distant eye, I find it most intriguing because these competing beliefs are gaining ground in our current climate, in which individualism is really winning. And in the larger society, there is a perception that there are only so many resources and opportunities to go around.

"All this leads people to believe that one has to find the best and groom the best for the few opportunities that exist—or are perceived to exist. Therefore competition is exacerbated because we have a context in which people believe that there is a scarcity, in which they believe they need to fight for those resources."

Can the premium currently placed on the value of individualism and competition shift to one that is more egalitarian? "We haven't even begun to tap into the intelligence that everyone has," Wheelock responded on a note of optimism that obviously fuels her work. "On the one hand, some people believe that there are only a few people who are very smart. Other people might say, 'In fact, we have only begun to tap the talents, skills, and abilities that we all have.' "

4

From Tracking to High-Quality Heterogeneous Instruction: Roger Genest

Pioneer Valley Regional District High School is a small rural consolidated high school in Northfield, Massachusetts that serves the four communities of Northfield, Bernardston, Warwick, and Leyden. Its current student population, which numbers approximately 567, is predominantly white. For the most part, parents work in the larger towns that surround the school district; some dairy farms are still in existence. Roger Genest, a veteran English teacher and chair of the English department, has been active in changing the school's instruction from homogeneity to heterogeneity. Formerly convinced that homogeneous instruction was the best way to reach students of differing achievement levels, today he is an advocate for heterogeneous instruction— and the cognitive and social shifts it demands. Genest began his teaching career at Pioneer Valley in 1963. He holds a bachelor's degree in English education from Keene State College and a master's degree from the University of Massachusetts.

When Pioneer Valley Regional District High School began its deliberate and conscious shift from homogeneous tracking to heterogeneous instruction in 1984, many school staff members were skeptics—if not absolute opponents—of the change. As Roger Genest is quick to explain, he was no exception. What he and

45

his fellow teachers could not foresee was that the change to heterogeneous instruction would become a tool with which they would
find it necessary to profoundly change their practice.

In talking to Roger Genest, one senses that the outcome of improved—considerably more demanding—instructional practices
has revitalized him professionally, a revitalization that he shares
with other school staff.

I asked: How and why did a shift to heterogeneous instruction
occur? What was your reaction to it when first proposed?

Genest's answer is one that is familiar to many who work in
schools and see reforms come and go with little lasting effect. "I
didn't see it as something my department would go along with,"
he admitted, "and I thought it would be forgotten like most of the
things that were talked about that were new at the time."

The Beginnings of Change

Pioneer Valley's prompt toward heterogeneity did not emerge
from a notion of equity, but from the concern of a guidance counselor who believed that changing to heterogeneous instruction
would better serve underperforming students and help them reach
their maximum potential. After the guidance counselor made her
initial presentation to the faculty, the idea of heterogeneous instruction quickly gathered momentum—to the point where Genest
became alarmed. In short order, a committee was appointed to
study the possibility of shifting Pioneer Valley's tracked instruction to heterogeneity.

"It became evident that this committee was going to have
some type of power, so I got a little nervous," he recollected. After
meeting with his colleagues in the English department, he discovered his trepidation was universal—and the consensus of his peers
was clear: Genest should serve on the committee as a "subversive."

"I joined the committee," he said, "and told them that I didn't
agree with the concept of the heterogeneous classroom and didn't
believe it would work at our school. We had a good principal who
responded by welcoming me to the committee. He made it clear
that they would listen to what I had to say and if I could prove that
it wouldn't work, they would go along with me. On the other

hand, if they proved to me that there would be a possibility that heterogeneous instruction would work I had to be as open-minded as they were."

Determined to sway the committee to his point of view, Genest began to buttress his argument against heterogeneous instruction by gathering information about schools that had already made the change. "I visited various schools," he said, "called various teachers who were supposedly involved in heterogeneous programs, and sent a series of letters to people who were researching heterogeneity. Within 6 weeks, I had collected quite a bit of information and felt comfortable going back to the committee and telling them that clearly this was not going to work."

In part, his conviction stemmed from observations that the schools he visited were shuffling students into different groups solely at the middle-track level with no change at the high and lower tracks—and claiming they were committed to truly heterogeneous instruction. "The schools I visited still had special programs for the students they perceived as remedial or low level," he observed, "and they had pull-out programs for advanced studies and honors programs."

Yet another large component of his opposition to heterogeneous instruction stemmed from a deeply held and sincere conviction that all students cannot be served by the same instruction—and when he visited schools that were maintaining homogeneous instruction albeit under a different name, he felt even more confident that heterogeneous instruction could not succeed.

When he reported his observations to the committee, they were directed to pursue discussions with teachers in their departments that would focus on what teachers believed was needed before they could consider seriously the possibility of heterogeneous instruction at Pioneer Valley.

Problems, Obstacles, and Solutions

What particular problems stood out? I asked. What, especially, did teachers fear? What, specifically, made them resistant to the idea of teaching heterogeneous classes?

"One problem was that teachers had no idea what to do if they were in heterogeneous classrooms," Genest said, "no idea what instructional methods needed to be used to teach kids. They saw no light at the end of this particular tunnel.

"Second, they felt that their training focused more on the individual rather than on an understanding of how heterogeneous instruction works."

These strongly held teacher beliefs assumed the timbre of a demand or, more plaintively, an entreaty, he reports. "The prevailing sentiment was: 'Show me how this is going to work.' "

When Genest reported to the committee the negative sentiments held by teachers within the English department, he was surprised to discover that their worries were universal among staff schoolwide. "Teachers felt comfortable in their classrooms but couldn't imagine how to change their teaching to accommodate heterogeneous grouping."

Realizing that the staff needed some help before undertaking any schoolwide change, Pioneer Valley's principal brought in a professor from the University of Massachusetts who was knowledgeable in planning and assessing curriculum—although he claimed no special knowledge of heterogeneous instruction. As an incentive, his class was offered at no charge to teachers, who received three graduate credits for taking it. This was a powerful motivation for teachers to enroll, Genest says.

During the course, teachers had the opportunity to try instructional methods that they had not previously used and be videotaped while experimenting with their classes. The videotapes were kept as nonthreatening as possible; staff had the option of receiving feedback or keeping the tapes solely for their own use. Genest, secure in his teaching, invited critical scrutiny of his first video, confident that he would provide a successful demonstration. As an additional challenge to his prowess as a teacher—and to test the premise of heterogeneous instruction—he decided not only to test a style of instruction unfamiliar to him but also to try it with a truly heterogeneous class.

"I took four of my honors students, four of my top academic students, four students from the general track, and four from my low-level track. I also asked the resource people to give me four students from special education, because at that time they were not mainstreamed into regular classes."

With the new variables of a different mode of instruction—coupled with a truly heterogeneous class—Genest was absorbed in ("and struggling with," he remembers) his instruction. The subtleties of classroom dynamics among the newly grouped students escaped him until he viewed the videotape—dynamics that had a great deal to do not only with homogeneous grouping and its effects but also with his mode of instruction.

"When I saw the video," he remembered, "I noticed that things weren't what I thought they were; instead, they were quite different."

One surprise was that students spontaneously seated themselves according to their prior academic groupings, with one honors student dominating all the discourse in the classroom. "He only spoke to his little group, never sharing the information with anyone. Actually, one of the low-track students understood the concept I was trying to get across, but it was quite noticeable that the high-track kids were not going to listen to what anybody else had to say.

"This one young honors student controlled the whole group. Everyone looked to him before they said anything. They looked for his approval—not my approval, but his approval. If he approved, then everything was okay."

Genest began to watch the student in his other class and noticed he was just as controlling in that setting. "He was the one who decided how much you were going to discuss that particular day."

With those preliminary observations in mind, he began another type of lesson: one in which students worked from an advanced organizer of information and then moved to a group discussion. "It didn't work," he stated simply. "The academic kids worked by themselves and weren't willing to share with the others in the class. When the honors student who dominated the discussion would talk, he couldn't explain what he was thinking to the students from lower-track classes. Instead, he used exactly my words rather than trying to find a way to communicate with his peers."

At that point, Genest was seized with the realization that he and his instruction were the problem. "What *I* was doing was the problem. My expectations for the kids and how I had trained them to act created a problem for them: They couldn't exchange information. I ended up giving them the text and asking them to teach it to me. I told them to forget everything I had told them; instead, I asked them to tell me what they found and what they thought about it."

The Moment of Change

The discussion that resulted was lively and sensible, as students began to comprehend the text in terms of their own experience. As Genest says, "For me that was the moment of truth." He began to ponder how well-intentioned teachers might accomplish the exact opposite of their goals—and remain convinced that they had done their utmost to help students.

Why? I asked.

As Genest replied, it became clear that the ability to observe one's own practice was an invaluable tool. "Many teachers didn't realize they were doing the things that they did in class. As an example, one of the videos of my instruction showed how my body language revealed exactly what I thought. It was obvious when I didn't agree with students. If someone finished a comment and I didn't agree, I just turned to someone else and started talking. The result was, of course, that the student I did that to immediately tuned out."

Were you shocked by your own behavior as a teacher? I asked.

"Yes, because I really didn't think I acted that way," he replied candidly. "One of the things that had come up in the course we took was that teachers can turn kids off. I didn't think I did—none of us did. I felt that I gave each student an opportunity to talk during class, and I listened to what each had to say. But when I viewed my classes on tape, it was very obvious that I had been encouraging kids to go along with what I thought. I ignored the kids who opposed me. I made it clear that they were off track."

Other teachers reacted in kind, and the review of videotapes—once regarded with little enthusiasm—began to be an occasion for teachers to get together in the evenings at each other's homes and discuss new ideas about teaching. "We were so excited watching ourselves and what was happening to us," Genest said simply. "Suddenly we were aware of what we were doing. People who weren't taking the course suddenly started listening and talking to us about what we were doing. By the end of the class, most of us were convinced that we at least wanted to try to teach heterogeneously."

Genest underscores the importance of Pioneer Valley's commitment to the change through their allocation of resources, allowing and encouraging staff to take risks in the classroom, and also promoting a climate in which evaluation was not a threat. "Our principal wanted us to try heterogeneous instruction," he pointed out, "it didn't cost us anything, and they gave us the time to experiment. They didn't get involved in a way that was threatening or critical to us."

Teaching Low-Track Students

Genest is particularly appalled when he reviews how well-intentioned—and misguided—instruction for low-track classes had been prior to the advent of heterogeneous grouping. "We felt we gave low-track kids every chance in the world," he mused. "We really went out of our way for them. We prepared special materials for them and felt we were doing the best we could. Of course, today any of us would laugh at that."

Were your expectations for low-track students clearly different than for academic-track students? I inquired.

"Totally different," he said. "For instance, I taught all 12th-grade English classes. My upper-level class went through the same materials that my lower class did, but in my upper-level class, I expected them to read on their own and come back to class to review the concepts. But in my low-level class, I would either show them a film or I would read the text with them. We would do everything in class, and I would lead them by the hand through the whole thing."

Genest's intentions were pure: If he exposed his low-track students to Shakespeare—although in a different way from his high-track students—he believed he had accomplished something significant. "I thought I was doing my low-track students a favor," he observed. "I used to complain, however, that they didn't have any concept of Shakespeare whatsoever. What I saw was that they couldn't do any high-level reading. Today I know that they weren't exposed to any high-level reading—or to any high-level thinking."

He added, "How can we expect kids to do higher level thinking if they have never been exposed to it?"

Accommodating individual differences is clearly the key, Genest believes, and one best accomplished in heterogeneous groups—not through tracked instruction that creates and separates groups from each other. "Not all kids are geared to reading and writing," he said. "Many kids learn visually and are able to break down a concept in a visual way that is quite sophisticated— far beyond what I could do."

Patience and Change

How long, I asked, did it take Pioneer Valley to shift from a tracked system to heterogeneous instruction? Once the process began, what were the steps away from tracking? How were they accomplished?

The change to heterogeneous instruction—which was synonymous with new instructional techniques—took years, with phases unfolding gradually. One way the change was eased was gaining the commitment of the veteran teachers, like Genest. Another was to require heterogeneous classes at the outset, with the accompanying option for all students that allowed them to take an accelerated class for at least half the year.

Over the first few years, teachers witnessed a drop in the numbers of students who opted for the accelerated courses—to the point that at the end of the third year, no freshmen enrolled in the accelerated program. As one student told Genest, "The real stuff is going on in the other classes. I get to see a lot of different views about things, and I learn a lot."

How, specifically, did instruction change? I asked. What did you learn to do differently?

Genest reports that his own instruction changed from an emphasis on coverage to a project-oriented approach. Yet, 3 years into the program, he was still perturbed by students' disengagement from academic material. After a sabbatical spent researching how students in remedial placements learn, he returned with a different attitude. "If a student can't exchange with other students what she knows, that is not a good academic student. Many teachers, of course, feel that if the kids do the work, and do it to their liking, they are excellent students."

Taking chances in the classroom became paramount, Genest emphasizes, and the key was for teachers to find what they loved to teach—an idea many had abandoned along the way because of the press to cover material. As teachers began to unlock their personal visions of education, Pioneer Valley's administration simultaneously encouraged the development of project-oriented curriculum by paying teachers to work through a summer developing a prototype of a new curriculum.

This curriculum development project, coupled with the laborious process of gaining schoolwide approval to institute it, resulted in changing the actual mechanics of teaching. As Genest explains, "Instead of teaching only 12th grade, we decided that all English teachers would teach at all levels. For instance, I would teach 9th, 10th, 11th, and 12th grade—as would all teachers.

"But we agreed that we needed to watch the process of the kids' growth. We didn't see that if we stayed within our grade levels. We also needed to identify those skills that were necessary at each grade level. We needed to know what kids needed to know and be able to do by the end of the school year."

Genest describes his classroom today. "My class size runs about 15 to 18 students," he says. "I begin by dividing the class into groups, with a specific task related to a text that we are studying. Each group presents what they discovered and whatever they processed that particular day. After presenting this to the whole group, we then have a group discussion."

He added, "This sounds easy but it is a long process."

Using a frequently taught text, *The Bad Seed*, he elaborates what he means. "Before we could even look at the book, we began by discussing what we believed about evil. Are there different types of evil? If there are different types of evil, how would you define those types of evil? It typically takes us about 2 weeks to agree on the different types of evil. In the process of defining them, they start to notice the difference between subjective and objective kinds of information."

"There are no lectures of any kind," he said. "There is a lot of individual work, group work, and oral presentations that is based on some type of research. I don't come in and talk about the book. They talk about the book."

He added, "The hard part is for me to keep still. We find it very difficult—but very important—to let the kids go through their own thinking process. Once they have completed it, we can present what various experts say, and we can solicit their input by asking how their thinking compares to students' beliefs about the text."

Gains in Achievement

Although the improvement in the numbers of students who go on to college cannot be attributed solely to the change to heterogeneous instruction, Genest takes obvious pride in the fact that prior to the shift in instruction, about 32% to 38% of Pioneer Valley's students entered college, compared to the current figures of 87% to 90%. Scores on standardized achievement tests remain constant, however.

Beyond the academic realm, other gains can be seen. "We don't have cliques in school anymore," he said. "Students help one another, they work together and respect one another's thinking. No one puts somebody down because of the way that they do things."

Perhaps the most telling testimony was provided by former Pioneer Valley students who returned to take part in a school-sponsored conference on heterogeneous instruction in 1990. "The panel of students was made up of young people who had experience in the low group or the resource room. They talked about how they felt today versus how they felt back when they were students. Every one of their comments accentuated what a positive development this was for our students."

5

Detracking With
Democratic Values:
Anna Hunderfund

Anna Hunderfund is Assistant to the Superintendent for Curriculum and Instruction in the Jericho Free Union School District in Jericho, New York. As principal of Jericho High School (1987–1990) and Middle School (1990–1993), she was instrumental in guiding the middle school to implement a research-driven plan to detrack the school's classes. Prior to entering school administration, Hunderfund taught Spanish literature at the high school level and then became a coordinator of talented and gifted students. A passionate advocate for detracking schools, Hunderfund holds a bachelor's degree from American University, a master's degree from the State University of New York at New Paltz, and an Ed.D. in educational administration from Teachers College, Columbia University.

Anna Hunderfund has a personal anecdote she tells that both illustrates and explains her passionate commitment to detracking schools in favor of heterogeneous instruction: her own incorrect placement in a track that might have led to a truncated future.

As Hunderfund explains, "My maiden name was Fernandez. I grew up in New Jersey, and did very well in grammar school—all the way through the eighth grade. My father had a third-grade education and my mother died midway through my freshman year in high school. There really was no one to navigate for me at that time.

"When I got to the high school, it had 3,000 students and, although I did not know it at the time, was divided into wings: vocational, commercial, and academic. I went to my first English class, which was in the vocational wing, and along the way I noticed that there were signs that said that everyone who entered here should be very careful. This was the first thing that I thought was odd.

"The kids looked really tough. I didn't have a leather jacket and I thought: I'd better get a whole new wardrobe! We were told to keep quiet and we wouldn't get into any trouble.

"When I went to my class, the teacher talked about the definition of a noun and the definition of a verb. As boring and elementary as I believed her instruction to be, I never thought that the inappropriate level of her instruction was the function of my placement. Instead, I thought it was the function of the teacher and the school.

"Within a few days I went to my homeroom teacher and told him I was really confused! I said: 'I have an English teacher who is the worst teacher that I've ever had in my life.' The teacher asked what the English teacher was teaching and I explained that she was teaching about nouns and verbs. My homeroom teacher looked at my schedule and said, 'I think there's been a mistake. You need to go to a guidance counselor.' "

Hunderfund remembers her visit to the guidance counselor especially because the high school's physical separation into wings was so pronounced and symbolic. "I went over a bridge into another place, sort of like being in another land, and introduced myself to the guidance counselor. After I explained my situation, she asked me: 'Who knows that you're here? Do your parents know?' She seemed very concerned about who might know I was visiting her. I said that they didn't know. She looked very flustered, and told me she was sorry. She had seen my last name and wasn't sure how well I spoke English."

Hunderfund exclaims, recollecting the situation: " 'You didn't know how well I spoke English? I was born in and never left this country!' And she told me, 'We had you down for a cosmetology major.' I told her I intended to go into the foreign service, and she told me she'd take care of it. I went *immediately* from cosmetology, which was in a terrible, ugly classroom, to an academic wing that was beautiful, that had wonderful teachers, to upper-level courses.

"I cannot explain to you the difference between the vocational wing and the academic wing," she added. "Obviously, I have never forgotten it. There was a bridge between the commercial and the academic wings, but there was nothing between the commercial and the vocational wings. There were only metal doors with signs on them that listed cautions about where you were going.

"The point," she emphasized, "is that had I not had the presence of mind to do that, it would have ruined the future that I had planned for myself. I was simply judged by my last name, not even by my records, not even by my scores on standardized tests or even how I looked or sounded. She saw my last name—and on the basis of that, determined my fate."

Detracking: One School's Process

This early experience, and her subsequent beliefs about differentiation, tracking, and sorting, came into sharp focus when Hunderfund came to Jericho Junior High School as its principal in the mid-1980s. At that time her task was to facilitate the transition from a traditional junior high for Grades 7–9 to a research-based, 6–8 middle school. "That is the process that prompted the research that we did on students' needs and the role of tracking," she explained.

Many would describe Jericho as an affluent suburb of New York City located on Long Island, with a fairly homogeneous student population characterized by affluence and privilege. As Hunderfund says, "The pressure here has less to do with going to college than it does with which college students will attend. We have very high parent expectations; parents are very well-educated and many are very affluent. Ninety-nine percent of our students go on to 2- and 4-year institutions.

"Because of the high socioeconomic status of the community, we can predict," she continued, "that most children in this community are going to achieve at high levels, almost despite what the schools do. The question is: How much higher can we get them to perform and on what measures other than traditional ones? Our public is a very critical group of individuals—and I mean that in the best way. They bring a tremendous amount of very knowledgeable scrutiny to what we do and say."

Although Jericho's students have few apparent disparities socioeconomically or racially, a careful examination of inschool practices revealed what Hunderfund calls "the human need to discriminate."

As one example, honors classes at Jericho Junior High School were instituted a year before Hunderfund arrived, as a response to considerable political pressure brought to bear upon the schools by parents who believed their children were insufficiently challenged. As she helped to facilitate the process that ultimately shifted the school both to a middle school and to a heterogeneously grouped school, her strategy was careful and deliberate: She would not respond to the tracking issue as a separate issue but instead would engage—with faculty and the community—in scrupulous study of the research on adolescent development to discover what schooling practices would best engage middle school students.

She recalled, "For the next 3 years, the faculty, the community, and I engaged in a very comprehensive research study about the developmental needs of middle school youngsters. I urged that we not start with solutions until we had really identified those needs which were developmentally appropriate for the children. I knew that whatever we were going to do educationally was going to be unsound if we didn't base it on students' developmental needs."

One pressing need the group identified linked to ego development—and the negative effects of competition. "We saw how fragile children's egos really are at the middle school age and how destructive competition is for many students. It was illogical to put them in highly competitive situations, whether in athletics or academics. Consequently, the middle school should be a time of exploration for them without the pressure and stress of extreme specialization that awaited them at the high school level."

Hunderfund reports that what she terms "my own bias" was reaffirmed by what school staff discovered in the research. "With my previous experience at the high school level, I had learned that unfortunately what we often refer to as student achievement has less to do with insight and significant ability—as measured by out-of-school kinds of measures—as it does with the ability to be a good test taker who is willing and able to conform to behavioral expectations."

The process away from differentiation to multiability instruction was not smooth. Teachers at many points along the way resisted the move to heterogeneous grouping, something that Hunderfund understands. "Many times the only models that we have in education are what we ourselves experienced. Our own teachers may not have done things on the basis of research but on the basis of the models available to them."

Yet when the faculty studied the research, they were the ones who took the initiative to suggest change, Hunderfund says. "Interesting and refreshingly," she noted, "they actually said that it would be very hard for them to justify or recommend the continuation of tracking on the basis of the research about it and about middle school children's developmental needs. As we discussed many of these educational issues, our weekly faculty meetings were not always pleasant experiences. Some of them were emotional situations.

"But eventually teachers realized that my intention was to ask: What is it that we consider to be the most important learning that should occur in this institution? Are there valid reasons for it? How can we make sure that we facilitate that learning for children in the most effective and efficient way possible?"

Yet the process of converting tracked instruction to heterogeneous classes was far from easy, she emphasizes. "At one point, the faculty was in favor of a differentiated honor roll: high, medium, and low."

Her tone of voice gives ample testimony to what she thought of that proposition. "My final words to them on this topic were that this honor roll ratio was an experiment I would go along with grudgingly and with the understanding that if this was something to which we wanted to subject the children, then it was something to which we would subject ourselves. In other words, when I supervised them and wrote their evaluations, I would use the same protocol that they would use with children.

"Only some teachers would be 'outstanding,' " Hunderfund recalled with some amusement, "and the majority would be a nebulous mass. I would make sure that we balanced the curve and that a certain percentage of teachers would not succeed because of our exceedingly high standards."

After an initial outcry—a heated protest—against her stance, teachers returned to the next faculty meeting and declared that this way of evaluating teachers would encourage competition, be destructive to group morale, and would lower their self-esteem and would promote dysfunctional group behavior. "To which," Hunderfund remembered, "I said: 'Precisely. And if, with your high levels of education and maturity, you have difficulty with this, why in the world would we subject 12- and 13-year-olds to the very same pathologies?' "

Instead, the differentiated honor roll was dropped, and in its place, the school decided to recognize children for their accomplishments in 12 areas, one of which was academic achievement. "It is important to note," Hunderfund points out, "that we did not approach the issue of tracking as an issue in and of itself, but instead looked at it in the context of students' needs. If we had approached it by itself, given the history and context in this community, it would have been a big issue politically. Instead, it was part of a whole analysis of what we were doing and what we valued in learning."

Changing Attitudes Toward Instruction

As part of the process of self-scrutiny, teachers had to relinquish long-held beliefs about how instruction should proceed. "If, in fact," Hunderfund added, "what we're trying to impart to children has more to do with being a whole individual as opposed to a computer that spits out data, then we have a responsibility to analyze very carefully the processes that we put into place, the procedures that reflect those processes, and the philosophies that generate the processes that prompt the procedures."

Hunderfund defines tracking not so much as a structural mechanism that allows the differentiation of curriculum and instruction to students but rather as something more insidious, a philosophy that sorts and ranks students by their perceived abilities—in the process destroying possibilities for their futures.

"One thing about tracking is that once you accept its philosophy about sorting children, lots of implications follow. Once you take the first step, you're in for the whole ride," she stated.

In what ways did teachers' practice begin to diverge from previous practice once Jericho Middle School moved to heterogeneous instruction? I inquired. In her reply, Hunderfund pointed to remedial instruction, the school's grading system, the role of scheduling, and student participation or nonparticipation in athletics to illustrate the far-reaching effects of tracking.

"In our school, we had a resource room not only for classified youngsters but also for children who required more time to acquire whatever the knowledge and skills were that were valued at that particular time. As noble as that was, and as really necessary as it was, when we started to analyze the implications of pulling children out of their classes, we saw no logic to it. The other part of the problem with remedial programs is that they are not interwoven into the curriculum, but are separate and different.

"It feels really good to say that I have lots of wheelchairs, and that I have given out wheelchairs to everyone who I think has any difficulty walking. While that sounds really noble and really wonderful, if I don't know what I'm doing, I undermine a lot of people who really do know how to walk. In fact, I destroy their ability to walk in the long run because their muscles are going to atrophy in the chair."

As faculty began to concur with these sentiments, more and more students were pushed into the mainstream, she says. "We also moved from a numerical grading system to a letter system; rather than giving Fs we gave Incompletes."

Next came a complete reconsideration of what to do with children who needed extra help without pulling them out of classes. "Our first solution was to pull them out of classes that were considered as less significant, such as the arts. But then we asked: How does that reinforce the holistic approach we want to have toward children as human beings?

"As we considered other solutions, the next possibility was not to schedule lunch for students who needed extra help. No lunch!"

she said with obvious disgust. "This unacceptable practice is more common than people realize."

Some of these solutions, she suggests, are completely destructive and can have significant deleterious effects. "If a child isn't doing well in math, he is taken out of art. Instead, he is scheduled for remedial math, sometimes in addition to his other math class. Rather than taking math in a way that is appropriate to his learning style and to the different notions of multiple intelligences, we give remedial math to the child in a more boring, repetitive, terrible, and grueling way. If there are deficits in several areas," she added with some vigor, "we take the child out of all his elective areas so that he is left with no areas of personal interest or perceived ability.

"Another solution might be to appease the child's parents by allowing the child to eat lunch while he does the work, so that he is deprived completely of socialization. If he has low self-esteem, concentration problems, or his learning style really requires interaction in order for him to learn, then placing him in a highly structured and isolated setting that is completely dominated by a teacher is totally inappropriate."

She noted, "We ruled out all of those options, I am happy to say. But it is important to note that if these questions weren't asked, discussed, and answered, these things would have happened by default."

The questions asked extended even to students' participation in athletics and cheerleading, she said. "Although the research on interscholastic sports at the middle school level was hard to locate, we did find studies from universities in Indiana, Michigan, and Texas. These studies showed that there were many fallacies that riddled the whole concept of competitive sports at the middle school level, especially pertaining to the way students were sorted and separated.

"The inequity of athletics and related programs, such as cheerleading, was also an issue. In a community such as this, a lot of families are traditional. There is both a mom and a dad in the house; the mom frequently stays home. But even here, depending on the interest and the time that parents have, a child might never learn how to play any particular sport. So is it our role, at the middle school level, to sort them and eliminate them from what might be a wonderful lifelong pursuit just because they may not come to us with the appropriate skills?"

Instead, Jericho worked to open up athletics and cheerleading to encourage more students to try out for teams—and their initiative was rewarded with the opportunity to participate. "The first year, a quarter of the school turned out for the cheerleading squad. As a result, we had 137 cheerleaders. The athletic director," she recalled with visible amusement, "wanted to know what he was going to do with all these kids. My reply was: 'Think of the number of spectators we will have when we rotate the kids.'

"We had kids who would probably end up as a valedictorian next to kids who were severely learning disabled next to the future homecoming queen next to someone who was probably going to be lucky if she got to go to the prom. There certainly were issues that the kids had to learn about taking orders, about practicing, and about the length of practice. It worked—we ended up with multiple teams in all sports. In fact, our high school has never had better athletic performance on teams than they do now, because they have so many more students from whom to draw.

"This shows," she said, "that tracking doesn't just pertain to academics. Tracking extends to much, much more."

Hunderfund returns to her chief concern, which she frames as the insidious and problematic nature of tracking's philosophy. "Some people believe that tracking simply refers to the classification of different classes. But it is much more insidious. If we are to talk about this in a substantive manner, we have to look at it in a much more philosophical context. Part of the problem lies in the fact that if we can be quasi-scientific about what we're doing—and assign numbers to it—it takes on a certain legitimacy."

Jericho's move to a sixth grade opened her eyes to how pervasive tracking can be throughout the grade levels—not solely at the secondary level. "I thought that the sorting of students was much more a secondary concept. I never realized that elementary grades can do it in a much more covert way. They have little reading groups and little math groups, with names for each of them, but the composition of the groups never changes."

The Lasting Effects of Tracking

What was the greatest surprise to you, I asked, throughout the move to hetereogeneous instruction?

"I suppose," Hunderfund replied thoughtfully, "how strong the notion of sorting really is in our society—and how, necessarily, that is what we reflect in school. I was also surprised by how illogical so much of it is, and how the basis for much of it could never be defended on a logical basis."

She concludes with a story. "I dealt with one child in particular quite a while ago who had been tracked into all non-Regents classes, which for some in New York City is considered 'at best to provide a minimal competency education.' In applying for admission to the Gifted and Talented program which I coordinated, the student did not qualify on the basis of IQ tests. Had I not pushed for and been granted permission to use other forms of assessment—such as portfolios and other documentation that attested to the fact that the student had the ability to accomplish what he said he wanted to do—he would not have been admitted to the program. At that point, we didn't have other forms of assessment.

"As it turned out, he wrote a grant which was funded by the National Endowment for the Humanities, in the amount of $2,000 to $3,000. At the time, he was a freshman in high school. For his grant, he documented that many Ph.D.s had drawn erroneous conclusions about a mining settlement in Orange County, New York, conclusions about why it had ceased to function. He ended up producing a huge document to the Board of Education that went on to the National Endowment for the Humanities, and he went from non-Regents classes to all honors classes."

But that arrangement was not satisfactory to the student, she remembers. "It is very interesting how perception dictates ability. This student had the integrity and the character to refuse the placement in every subject except social studies. He went on to finish high school in 3 years. He finished his senior year of high school and his freshman year at Bard College simultaneously. He finished college in 3 years and went on to do Ph.D. work in archeology at Boston University."

His placement in non-Regents classes was dictated not only by his test scores but by his behavior, she emphasizes—a lesson she wants school people to learn and absorb thoroughly. "He was rebellious. He did not conform to the standard dress code at the time. He could be very antagonistic, very provocative in what he had to say. But when we turned to the research much later at Jericho Middle School, it reinforced for me the crazy things we do to kids, crazy things that often are done on the basis of inertia and because we do what was done to us."

Bibliography

Fiedler, E. D., Lange, R. E., & Winebrenner, S. (1993). In search of reality: Unraveling the myths about tracking, ability grouping and the gifted. *Roeper Review, 16,* 4-7.

Fordham, S., & Ogbu, J. U. (1986). Black students' school success: Coping with the "burden of 'acting white'." *The Urban Review, 18*(3), 176-206.

Gamoran, A. (1986). Instructional and institutional effects of ability grouping. *Sociology of Education, 59*(4), 233-243.

Gamoran, A. (1989). Measuring curriculum differentiation. *American Journal of Education, 97*(2), 129-143.

Gamoran, A. (1992). Access to excellence: Assignment to honors English classes in the transition from middle to high school. *Educational Evaluation and Policy Analysis, 14*(3), 185-204.

Gamoran, A. (1993). Alternative uses of ability grouping in secondary schools: Can we bring high-quality instruction to low-ability classes? *American Journal of Education, 102*(1), 1-23.

Gamoran, A., & Berends, M. (1987). The effects of stratification in secondary schools: Synthesis of survey and ethnographic research. *Review of Educational Research, 57,* 415-435.

Gamoran, A., & Mare, R. D. (1989). Secondary school tracking and educational inequality: Reinforcement, compensation, or neutrality? *American Journal of Sociology, 94,* 1146-1183.

Gamoran, A., Nystrand, M., Berends, M., & LePore, P. C. (1995). An organizational analysis of the effects of ability grouping. *American Educational Research Journal, 32*(4), 687-715.

Gardner, H. (1983). *Frames of mind: The theory of multiple intelligences.* New York: Basic Books.

Gardner, H. (1993). *Multiple intelligences: The theory in practice.* New York: Basic Books.

Glazer, N. (1987). In search of excellence and equity in our nation's schools. *Harvard Educational Review, 57*(2), 196-207.

Glazer, S. (1990, December 28). Why schools still have tracking. *Editorial Research Reports,* 746-759.

Hallinan, M. T. (1994). Tracking: From theory to practice. *Sociology of Education, 67*(2), 79-91.

Kirp, D. L. (1973). Schools as sorters: The constitutional and policy implications of student classification. *University of Pennsylvania Law Review, 121*(4), 705-797.

Kliebard, H. M. (1992). *Forging the American curriculum: Essays in curriculum history and theory.* New York: Routledge.

Kliebard, H. M. (1995). *The struggle for the American curriculum, 1893-1958* (2nd ed.). New York: Routledge.

Kozol, Jonathan. (1991). *Savage inequalities: Children in America's schools.* New York: Crown.

Lockwood, A. T. (1993). Multiple intelligences in action. *Research and the Classroom, 4.*

Lockwood, A. T. (in press). *Conversations with educational leaders: Contemporary viewpoints on education in America.* Albany, NY: SUNY Press.

Moore, D. R., & Davenport, S. (1988). *The new improved sorting machine.* Madison, WI: National Center on Effective Secondary Schools.

Oakes, J. (1983). Tracking and ability grouping in schools: Some constitutional questions. *Teachers College Record, 84*(4), 801-819.

Oakes, J. (1985). *Keeping track: How schools structure inequality.* New Haven, CT: Yale University Press.

Oakes, J. (1990). *Multiplying inequalities: The effects of race, social class, and tracking on opportunities to learn mathematics and science.* Santa Monica, CA: RAND.

Oakes, J. (1992). Can tracking research inform practice? Technical, normative, and political considerations. *Educational Researcher, 21*(4), 12-21.

Oakes, J. (1995). Two cities' tracking and within-school segregation. *Teachers College Record, 96*(4), 681-690.

Oakes, J., Gamoran, A., & Page, R. N. (1992). Curriculum differentiation: Opportunities, outcomes, and meanings. In P. W. Jackson (Ed.), *Handbook of research on curriculum* (pp. 570-608). Washington, DC: American Educational Research Association.

Ogbu, J. U. (1994). Racial stratification and education in the United States: Why inequality persists. *Teachers College Record, 96*(2), 264-298.

Page, R. N. (1990). Games of chance: The lower-track curriculum in a college-preparatory high school. *Curriculum Inquiry, 20*(3), 249-281.

Page, R. N. (1991). *Lower track classrooms: A curricular and cultural perspective.* New York: Teachers College Press.

Page, R. N., & Valli, L. (Eds.). (1990). *Curriculum differentiation: Interpretive studies in U.S. secondary schools.* Albany: SUNY Press.

Sapon-Shevin, M. (1994). *Playing favorites: Gifted education and the disruption of community.* Albany, NY: SUNY Press.

Slavin, R. E. (1990). Achievement effects of ability grouping in secondary schools: A best-evidence synthesis. *Review of Educational Research, 60*(3), 293-336.

Sleeter, C. E., & Grant, C. A. (1987). The impact of federal equity policies on a school: A case study. *Educational Policy, 1*(3), 355-373.

Sorgen, M. S. (1973). Testing and tracking in public schools. *The Hastings Law Journal, 24,* 1129-1190.

Wells, A. S., Hirshberg, D., & Lipton, M. (1995). Bounding the case within its context: A constructivist approach to studying detracking reform. *Educational Researcher, 24,* 18-24.

Wheelock, A. (1992). *Crossing the tracks: How "untracking" can save America's schools.* New York: The New Press.

Yeakey, C. C., & Bennett, C. T. (1990). Epilogue: Cultural reform and social struggle for a truly democratic society. *Journal of Negro Education, 59*(1), 86-97.

CORWIN
PRESS

The Corwin Press logo—a raven striding across an open book—represents the happy union of courage and learning. We are a professional-level publisher of books and journals for K–12 educators, and we are committed to creating and providing resources that embody these qualities. Corwin's motto is "Success for All Learners."